Y0-CTA-144

Introduction to Bait Fishing

a
STACKPOLE
BOOK

Introduction to Bait Fishing

RAY OVINGTON

INTRODUCTION TO BAIT FISHING

Copyright ©1971 by
THE STACKPOLE COMPANY
Published by
STACKPOLE BOOKS
Cameron and Kelker Streets
Harrisburg, Pa. 17105

All rights reserved, including the right to reproduce this book or portions thereof in any form or by any means, electronic or mechanical, including photocopying, recording, or by any information storage and retrieval system, without permission in writing from the publisher. All inquiries should be addressed to Stackpole Books, Cameron and Kelker Streets, Harrisburg, Pennsylvania 17105.

ISBN 0-8117-0911-6
Library of Congress Catalog Card Number 73-162447

Printed in U.S.A.

Contents

		Page
	Introduction	9
	Acknowledgment	11
	PART I	
	BAIT FISHING AS A SPORT	
1	**Why Fish with Bait?**	16
2	**Distinctions among Bait Types**	19
3	**Tackle Types**	22

Properly Balanced Tackle   Fly Fishing Gear
Spinning Gear   Baitcasting Gear
Regulation Saltwater Gear   Rigging and
Handling the Tackle   Handling the Tackle
for Casting   Terminal Tackle   Knots and
Hooks   Casting   General Bait
Presentation and Retrieves   Striking,
Playing, Landing

4 Fish of Most Interest to Sportsmen   53

Freshwater Species
   The Trouts   Pacific Salmon
   Freshwater Basses   Northern Pike,
   Muskellunge and Walleye Pike
   General Panfish   Other Panfish

Saltwater Species
   Striped, Channel Bass and Seabass
   Pollock, Cod and Bluefish
   Saltwater Panfish, Flounders, Porgies, etc.
   Weakfish and Sea Trout   Pompano,
   Jacks, Permit and Amberjack
   Snook and Tarpon   Boston, Spanish
   and King Mackerel   Bonefish, Ladyfish
   Tunas, Albacore and Bonito
   Marlin (Black, White, Striped,
   Blue)   Sharks   Barracuda
   and Cobia   Wahoo, Dolphin

PART II
FRESHWATER BAIT FISHING

5 Techniques for Catching Panfish   84

Bait Lake Stillfishing   Drifting, Casting,
Trolling   Ice Fishing   Introduce
Others to Fishing Pleasure

6 Bait Fishing Techniques   91
for Freshwater Game Fish

Large or Smallmouth Bass   Trout
Lake Trout and Walleye Pike
Pike and Musky   Steelhead

7 Bait Stream Fishing   105
   in Brook and Creek
     Baits that Catch Freshwater Fish
        Earthworms   Nightcrawlers
        Live Minnows   Dead Minnow
        Cut Bait   Aquatic Insects
     Land-bred Insects as Bait
     Unnatural Baits
     Terminal Rigs   Fishing Technique
     Drift Fishing   Stillfishing

8 Catching, Keeping and Carrying   122
   Live Bait
     Aquatic Insects   Other Aquatic Baits
     Live Minnows   Land-bred Insects

9 Freshwater Fishing Accessories   127
     Boating Fisherman

PART III
SALTWATER BAIT FISHING

10 Tides, Tackle and Bait   132
     Tides   Tackle   Baits for
     Saltwater Panfish   Natural Saltwater Baits
     and How to Rig Them   Saltwater Lines
     and Terminal Tackle   Special Knots
     for Saltwater Fishermen   Leaders for
     Saltwater Bait Fishing   Sinkers for
     Saltwater Fishing   Hooks for
     Saltwater Baits   Rods   Stillfishing
     Techniques   Trolling Techniques

11 Surf, Beach and Jetty Fishing   160
     Terminal Tackle for Beach and Jetty
     Trolling Beach and Jetty

12 Offshore Trolling for Big Game Fish   167
    Terminal Tackle for Offshore Fishing
    Equipping for Big Game Fishing
    Fishing Tackle and Terminal Gear
    Shark Fishing

FOR REFERENCE

Unhooking and Cleaning the Catch   180

Dictionary of Natural Baits   182

Glossary   191

Acknowledgment

THE AUTHOR'S HEARTFELT thanks to good friend, confidant and editorial savant, Peter Guttilla, for his unstinting assistance as several times given during the preparation of this book.

Introduction

THE PURPOSE OF this book is to offer helpful information on the use of natural baits in fishing. It covers the essentials in fishing for all the commonly sought fresh and saltwater species.

For those who have never fished before, I hope that the book will answer many questions: tackle selection and use; fishing techniques; the right bait offerings for various species under all fishing conditions; the how's and why's of rigging baits, sinkers, lines, floats, etc.; how to locate, preserve and attach natural baits correctly; what kind of terminal tackle to use and when. So it's all about natural bait fishing, right down to finally netting the fish.

For those who have fished before chiefly with artificial lures and flies, I hope that this presents bait fishing in a new light; namely, as being as much of a sporting proposition as fishing via the other methods.

For many years the authors of fishing books have centered their attention almost exclusively on fishing with artificial lures and flies, these methods being nearly always represented as the practice of angling in its highest sporting form. This is not so, because any sound concept of giving the fish a fair and sporting chance ought to embody more than dogmatically using an artificial lure. There is a whole lot more to good sportsmanship and sport in fishing than just that!

We have modeled or inherited much American angling tradition from the purists of latter-day Europe, especially relating to fly fishing for trout and salmon. In fact, there are even some "purists" who go to the extreme of suggesting that wet fly trout fisherman are more or less low-level dullards compared to the dry fly artist or, more accurately, perhaps, "addict."

While there is indeed much fun and sport in taking fish with artificial-lures-only, bait fishing can be its equal and, at times, its superior. It's been known to happen, for instance, that one can sometimes fish all day using artificial-lures-only, and not get a single rise or strike. Now how much sport is there in that, really, as compared to the possibility of turning a dull day into at least a modest success story simply by switching over to whatever natural bait is appropriate? And this without in any way departing from the standards of good sportsmanship.

The reason and need for this book is, no matter what kind of bait or lure is actually used, fishing secrets, as indeed there are, lie in the correct selection and skilful use of the

INTRODUCTION

right gear, baits and lures, taking into account the species sought and the conditions prevailing. Certainly no one is entitled to think that just because he chucks a worm overboard or casts a plug or fly he'll automatically connect with a lunker! There's a lot more to fishing than just that.

Regretable as it may be, there are quite a few dads today who are much at a loss when their youngsters suggest going fishing. Sometimes this is because they've never themselves fished, or perhaps they recall long-ago fumblings with hook and worm, watching others catch fish, yet returning home, their own stringers empty.

So, if one has never fished before, bait fishing is a great way to begin. Also, it happens to be the least expensive and least complicated way to fish! And it is a lot better, I propose, for new fisherman or young fisherman to start out that way, hopefully catching at least a few fish and thereby developing enthusiasm for fishing. Better, that is, than missing out on a lifetime of fishing fun purely through disappointment in fishing achievements using artificial lures or flies alone. The same, of course, might happen using natural baits; on the other hand, catching even some small fish with natural bait might whet one's interest.

In any case, for those who may someday dabble with lures and fly action along the way to becoming "the complete angler," bait fishing does offer invaluable experience.

Also, let's hope that through this book those who regard themselves as seasoned anglers, but who may have forgotten or by-passed the sport to be had in using natural baits, will find this information reviving their interest and bringing increased fishing fun.

But please understand this, there is nothing whatsoever in this book intended to deprecate fishing with artificial-lures.

Far from it; the sport of fishing is roomy enough for all—those who prefer that kind of fishing exclusively, those who prefer bait fishing, as well as the "in betweens," those who may alternate as conditions suggest.

In this day and age, the growing number of owners of small boats suitable for saltwater fishing zooms right along. There is fast access to surf and ocean beach for more and more fishermen through better highways. No wonder there is growing interest in saltwater fishing in which natural baits are very important. For such fishermen there is much in this book applicable to barge, beach, bay, pier, jetty, surf, small-boat and party-boat fishing, and even for those seeking bigger trophy fish far offshore.

Old-fashioned luck, of course, is always an underriding element in fishing. But there are ways to reduce the risk of coming home empty-handed; just another way of saying that in any form of fishing, going about it without some fundamental knowhow is utter nonsense!

Whether you are a seasoned fisherman or a novice, an old fisherman or a young one, there's much interesting and helpful detail in this book about baits and bait fishing—all intended to help you along the way to more fishing fun!

R.O.

PART I
BAIT FISHING AS A SPORT

1

Why Fish with Bait?

SOME FISH CAN only be caught with bait. Others can be taken with bait or lures, but all fish can be hooked with bait of the right kind, presented in the right way.

There is a mythical distinction perpetuated between bait and artificial lure fisherman—a distinction based on the picayunish orthodoxy which, in its snobbism, attempts to relegate bait fishermen as beneath the level of other sportsmen. This is inanity. The bait fisherman is every bit the sportsman that any other angler purports to be. Anyone who takes more than the legal limit of fish, or who kills fish not really needed or desired for food or trophy purposes is not really a sportsman, no matter what kind of enticer he uses.

Conservation directives are mandatory. Bait fishing is

WHY FISH WITH BAIT?

somewhat frowned upon in areas where heavy restrictions are placed on the number of fish one can catch. This is primarily due to the fact that natural bait fishing can be more efficient than fishing with artificial-lures-only, where the accent is placed on the sporting aspect of tactics and maneuvers rather than simply catching a fish. This is particularly true in freshwater trout fishing. The extreme of this is exemplified in Atlantic salmon angling; artificial flies only; unweighted; no bait nor metal lures of any kind used.

Why fish with bait?

Because it catches fish successfully and it is great fun.

Bait fishing offers the fish what it wants; the natural food upon which it feeds. The trick is to present it in the most natural way possible and with the most sporting tackle one can buy. This requires correct and balanced gear essential for casting the bait to the target as accurately and effortlessly as possible. The gear must be designed to handle the fish properly; be able to play the fish from weeds or snags; bring it up from the deep and yet still give the angler the full impact of exciting "fish action."

Bait is easily available and usually on the spot. There is no need to bring along tackle boxes filled with artificial lures. It is also much less expensive, since bait is free for the gathering or, even if purchased from bait liveries and tackle stores, it's still relatively inexpensive.

Though it may seem to many that successful bait fishing is a certainty or that such an angler will return home with fish every time, this is not necessarily true. The odds are in his favor, but there is never a guarantee. There is always the element of perfect technique and timing, the ability to hook, play and land the fish, but—beware, there can be many slips between the cup and the lip!

A live minnow is cast into a trout stream's current slick. The line is allowed to run off the reel after the cast. The minnow is carried along in the current swirls and sinks down to the rocks and gravel. A trout is there and it's hungry. It grabs the bait and the angler thrills to the action. A bass sitting on the bottom of a lake is offered a juicy earthworm from topside by an angler anchored over his lair. The bass may not be hungry, but its instinct to nibble is irresistible. It takes hold of the morsel and the battle begins.

Out on the big deep, a bonefish—stripped of its backbone and firmly shackled to a large hook—is dragged along the ocean's surface. Marlin—from 150 to 1000 lbs.—are in the vicinity. These are voracious feeders. One chunky marlin eyes the bait, following it cautiously as it trolls behind the cruiser. The big one finally takes hold and another angler gets the thrill of his life.

That's bait fishing! And it definitely is a sporting proposition.

Bait fishing terminal tackle requirements are a bit different as in rod action—or at least more critical in some instances than when fishing exclusively with artificial lures. The subject is covered in detail in chapter 3.

2
Distinctions among Bait Types

THERE ARE VARIOUS types of fishing bait, e.g., natural; resident; live; dead or cut; plus baits made from foods alien to fish but nonetheless tasty and effective.

Specific waters have indigenous baits which can be used on the hook to entice fish that ordinarily feed on them. The black bass, for example, is used to feeding on lake shiners, minnows and frogs which abound in its natural habitat, not omitting an occasional dinner on its own offspring. The brook trout finds insects living in rocks and gravel which are almost as abundant as, say, grass is to grazing cattle. The saltwater flounder sliding along the mud flats finds its way over clams and sea worms that simply delight its scaly underpinnings. Sailfish gather near schools of baitfish such as mullet, and slash into them with churning gusto.

The angler wishing to take these and the myriad of fresh and saltwater species of fish merely needs to gather the right bait and proffer it to the fish in a correct and natural manner. Such delivery will appear normal to the fish, whether it be a chunk of dead bait lazily drifting in the current, trolled along the surface behind the boat, or cast a short distance by rod.

In order to classify and describe the various baits and their presentation, the baits are divided into certain categories. There are natural baits deriving from specific waters and these may comprise—as in streams—aquatic or waterborne insects which spend their entire existence in the water save a few days airborne shore leave. There are also aquatic minnows, shellfish, frogs and worms. Other natural baits include land-bred insects and animal life that find their way to the stream, namely moths, crickets, grasshoppers, earthworms and caterpillars, etc. The same types throng in and about the lakes. In the ocean, all food for fish is contained in the ocean, itself, and constantly in reach of both angler and fish. Examples: shrimp, squid, sea worms, crustaceans, minnows, small school fish and occasionally even game fish.

These are the natural bait and they are presented in various ways, e.g., live and/or dead on a hook; dead on a hook and rigged in special ways such as cut in small or large sections and arranged, etc. In some instances of saltwater angling, a chumline is established in the fishing area by grinding up bait that is used on a hook, it is then tossed into the water gradually as the boat moves along forming a "slick," which will attract schools of the desired sport fish.

DISTINCTIONS AMONG BAIT TYPES

The last, and equally important category is that of unnatural baits, those made of food materials not found in the waters, but combined or concocted by man expressly for the fish. These are used more specifically for catfish and carp and for these fish extra-smelly baits are very effective; the smellier the better. Cheese and corn are great trout-takers despite the fact that such would be completely strange to the fish in their natural environment. Porkrind, a piece of meat and fat from a pork roast, is one of the best baits discovered for freshwater fish such as bass and pike.

There is almost as much natural bait variety as there are fish species and a variety of fishing conditions where appropriate natural baits can be selected. It is an expansive picture filled with many alternatives that can provide fishing fun for those interested in giving fish exactly what they want. The equally important factor, that of tackle balance and technique, will be considered, too, in upcoming chapters.

3
Tackle Types

THERE ARE LITERALLY hundreds of combinations of tackle used on various species of fish under all conditions of fresh and saltwater angling. There are specific *types* of tackle also used. Terminal gear, or the "business end" of the line includes swivels, sinkers, leaders, hooks and bait rigs, all of equal importance and many in number and quality.

The choice of these elements is not difficult or complicated. Most important is to select tackle that is easy to handle. Not all people have the same "feel" for fishing gear any more than they do for tennis racquets, golf clubs or sports cars. There can be variances between rod weights and lengths, for example, to fulfill the same project. Conditions

TACKLE TYPES

also enter the picture. If one is casting a trout stream and desires long casts, one rig is needed. On the other hand, the same rig may not be at all ideal when fishing a small brook. Flounder bottom fishing can be done without a rod, while fishing for marlin and sailfish requires a considerably strong rod and reel with large line capacity.

Where the art of casting is involved, the combination of rod, reel, line, leaders and terminal weights and hooks has to be balanced. Too light tip action in a rod will not allow casting a heavy weight; too strong a tip action will tend to flip the bait off on the cast.

PROPERLY BALANCED TACKLE

In order to catch fish with bait or artificial lures, proper tackle is a must. This can consist of very simple inexpensive equipment, or it can be a rig quite involved and costly. The best advice that can be given is to use first-rate tackle, yet it doesn't have to be the most expensive. A simple hand line; store string, a metal bolt or screw, or even a stone for weight and a penny hook will suffice in simple fishing. But tackle can also involve extremely heavy reels, miles of line, expensive rods and fighting chairs totaling well over a thousand dollars. The wrong decision can be made in choosing simple tackle as easily as with the most complex. There is no practical reason or need to do so if the facts are known.

Fishing tackle was originally designed as a result of man's desire and need to catch fish for food. Sporting gear is merely tackle refined to produce the most action and allow sporting principles to prevail in fishing; it serves to deliver the bait accurately and effortlessly, be it light and small, or big and heavy.

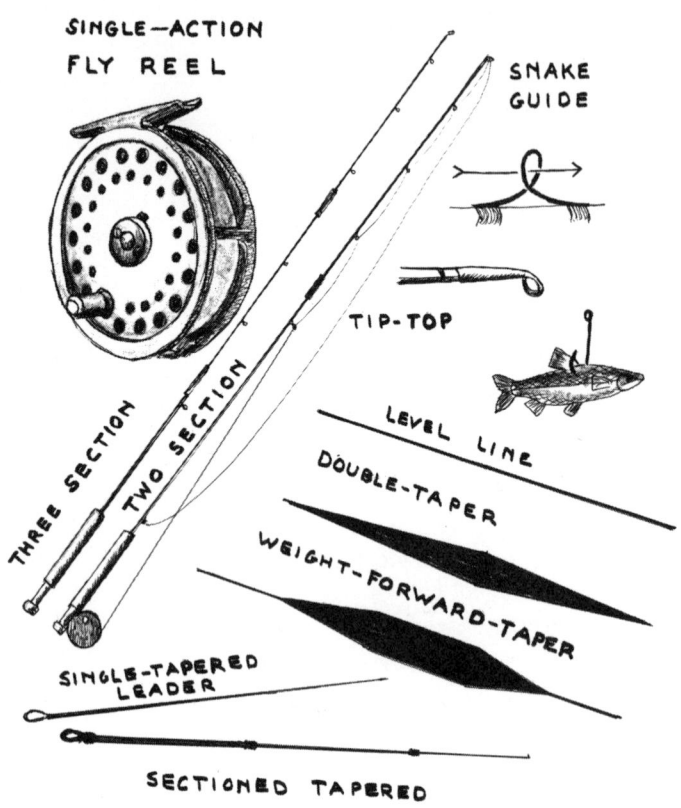

This is a typical fly reel, rod and line, rigged as it should be. The rods come in two or three-piece sections, depending on length. Reel is single-action. Line is tapered and its thickness is determined for balance; there are several kinds of line for fly rods, each to suit some specific casting purpose.

TACKLE TYPES

Visit a tackle store. Make friends with the proprietor and discuss local fishing needs. Talk with experienced anglers; watch them fishing and note their tackle and its use. But be prudent in buying. Cheap tackle can be an abomination and a waste of money. It is better to buy well-known brands names rather than something that "looks just as good at half the price." Good tackle, well cared for, will last many years and give dependable service.

Extra-heavy line is unnecessary and difficult to cast; extra-light line will break too easily and fail to get the bait to its destination. A heavy weight cannot be cast at all with flimsy rod action. The reel should be chosen to make casting as effortless as possible and contain enough line of sufficient strength (pound test).

Let's assemble combinations to fit specific fishing conditions and fish species.

FLY FISHING GEAR

Fly rods and reels are specifically designed to cast very light flies and lures. This tackle is also excellent for bait fishing in both fresh and saltwater. The fly rod looks like the one in the illustration; the reel is *behind* the hand and, for the most part, functions only to hold the line. Except with very big fish in fast water, the fish is seldom "played" from the reel; the line control is manipulated by hand in harmony with the bend of the rod. In spinning and baitcasting, the fish is played from the reel and the cast lure is controlled directly by the action of the reel.

Fly rods come in two or three-piece sections. Bamboo was the most practical material until the advent of fiberglas. Fly reels are of single action, meaning there is no "gearing up" as in baitcasting or spinning reels. One turn of the handle means one turn of the spool. Some fly reels have line drags or "brakes" that are adjustable for pressure and line control as well as for playing the fish (in the case of big game fish, fly reels used for bonefish, salmon and the like).

Fly lines are designed in three styles: level, double-tapered and weight-forward or bullet-tapered for long-distance "shoot casting." The latter is seldom used in bait fishing. The most practical line for our purposes here is the level line (either floating or sinking) for close-in work or, at the most, a double-tapered line for casting extremely light weights long distances and usually made of braided nylon.

Fly fishing tackle must be balanced. The reel must not be too heavy, the line neither too light nor too heavy.

Follow the accompanying chart for the selection of balanced fly tackle for both fresh and saltwater fishing.

SPINNING GEAR

The spinning outfit is by far the most versatile combination of rod, reel and line, and it is used extensively in casting and trolling baits for both fresh and saltwater fishing. The ultralight spinning combinations can be used for small trout and panfish baits, the medium freshwater weights are adequate for most species including pike and musky fishing. These last require heavier rods, stiffer actions and heavier lines. They are also excellent for saltwater species up to and including the sailfish, so one rig can be used interchangeably. Most medium-weight spinning gear can be used in both waters for comparable fish.

The spinning rod and reel are assembled as in the illustration with the reel (open-faced type) hanging down in the

RECOMMENDED TACKLE FOR FLY FISHING

FISH SIZE AND CONDITIONS	ROD LENGTH	ROD ACTION	LINE SIZE	AFTMA	REEL SIZE
Small trout, panfish, small streams, ponds.	6 1/2' (Short, lightweight, used only for very small, light baits, short casts.)	Dry Fly Medium	C- HCH, HCF	6	Small
Same, with bigger fish.	8 1/2'	Medium	B-GBG-GBF	7	Medium
Longer casts, heavier baits.	8 1/2' (Good for bait fishing fast streams because of a little more backbone and power when using heavier baits for fighting fish in strong currents.)	Dry Fly	B-GBG-GBF	7	Medium
Long distance, heavy baits, fresh and salt-water fishing.	9' (Considered the bass bugging rod, it is well adapted to baitfishing for every fresh and saltwater species, including bonefish and tarpon.)	Bass Bug	GAF	8	Heavy Large Cap.
Long distance, heavy winds, big baits, big fish.	9 1/2 to 10' (Anything up to muskellunge, tarpon.)	Heavy	G3AF	10	Heavy Large Cap.

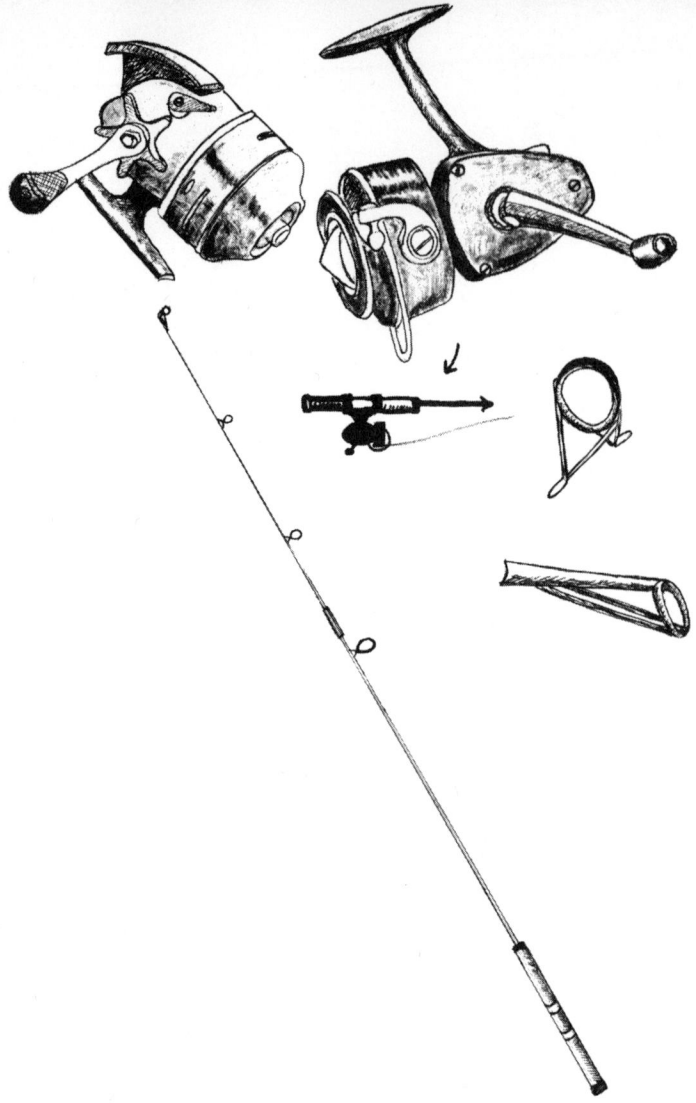

Note the spinning rod's long handle and the large guides. The spinning reel is usually mounted below the rod handle rather than above it as is the case with most baitcasting combinations. Reel at upper left may be mounted and used either above or below the rod handle.

center of the rod handle, and closed-face reels are used above or below as shown. The line guides are bigger than on the fly or baitcasting rods because the line comes off the end of the reel spool in coils. The handle is equipped with an anti-reverse gear so it will not spin around, but will activate the adjustable drag. The rods are generally two-piece and preferably glass. The preferred line is monofilament nylon. It can vary in weight from one-pound to forty-pound test. Rods extend from four feet to nine as in the case of big surfcasting tips.

The main advantage of spinning gear is that it enables the angler to cast extremely lightweight baits great distances when the tackle is balanced. There is no danger of "backlash" or reel line tangle due to overspinning of the reel spool as frequently happens with conventional baitcasting reels. The spinning spool is stationary; the line is pulled over the end as needed rather than over the revolving bale.

Again, balance is necessary for the project at hand. To cast an unweighted worm in a small stream requires a light, soft-action rod and light line. To fling a dead shrimp far into the surf requires a heavy rod, big reel with large line capacity and a heavy line and sinker rig.

The accompanying chart can be a useful reference and guide.

BAITCASTING GEAR

Baitcasting gear was designed 100 years ago as a simple crank, spool, pole and line. It has been refined a good deal since and has become the most popular casting outfit for both artificial lure use and baitcasting—especially in cases of freshwater bass, pike and trout. It was basically refined in

RECOMMENDED TACKLE FOR SPINNING

FISH SIZE AND CONDITIONS	ROD LENGTH	ROD ACTION	LINE TEST	LURE WEIGHT	REEL SIZE
Panfish, small trout, quiet waters.	6' (Designed for catching smallest game and panfish, yet capable of handling bigger ones in open water. Very sporting.)	U/LT	2-6 lbs.	1/16 to 1/4 oz.	Ultra Light
Small fish, fresh and saltwater.	6 1/2' (A bit larger than above for heavier baits, longer casts and tidal or stream currents.)	LT	2-6 lbs.	1/8 to 3/8 oz.	Small
Bass, pike, small tarpon, sea trout.	7 1/2' (Conventional level-wind reels can also be used and are preferred by steelheaders and big-fish anglers of the South.)	SE	4-12 lbs.	1/4 to 3/4 oz.	Small Medium Cap.
Striped bass, pike, musky, med. saltwater fish.	7' 9" (A standard two-handed rod for light saltwater and heavy steelhead baiting, live shrimp popping, up to big tarpon.)	MED	10-30 lbs.	1 to 3 oz.	Medium
Surf, most big lakes, big freshwater fish, med. saltwater fish.	9' (The surfer's favorite, also for jetty fishing; also used for cod, pollock, grouper, sea bass, cobia, amberjack, with heavy sinkers and terminal gear.)	MED	10-25 lbs.	1 to 3 oz.	Medium Large Cap.

Legend:
U/LT	Ultra-light	V/HVY	Very heavy	UFT	Ultra-fast taper
LT	Light	MED	Medium	FT	Fast taper
LTM	Light-medium	HVY	Heavy	SE	Salmon egg

TACKLE TYPES 31

rod types for trolling, casting and particularly surf long-distance casting. Its adherents swear by it to this day despite the advent of spinning gear and, although it diminished in popularity for a time, it's currently regaining its proper place in the fishing scene.

As shown, the baitcasting reel is mounted above the handle and the rod is either one or two-piece, joining at the handle or butt section and tip. The reel is the multiplying type, four turns of the spool to one turn of the handle for quick line retrieve. A level-wind bar travels back and forth across the reel spool to distribute the line evenly for the next cast. There are two types of controls for drag; the star or the button. Line is generally of braided nylon, though some anglers use the monofilament line with equal zeal.

Balance is the "must" key here. For bait fishing, a softer tip on a longer rod is required; a shorter, stiffer-tipped rod is generally used for throwing heavy artificial lures. It can be used for trolling as well as casting, though a shorter tip is frequently better for trolling. The saltwater boat rod is a variation of the typical freshwater trolling rod. The surf rod, a big double-handed rod with a long tip, is used for distance casting from beach, jetty or boat.

Several categories are shown in the accompanying charts for this most versatile fishing set-up. Choose tackle for the job at hand.

Recommendations here should be checked out in the light of local conditions at a local tackle store where one can discuss his personal bait fishing needs with competent tackle salesmen—men *who fish themselves,* and talk reality rather than sales pitches and theory. Look over the tackle. Get the "feel" of the rod actions and become acquainted with the reels and lines. Then it will be time to consider the terminal

RECOMMENDED TACKLE FOR BAITCASTING

FISH SIZE AND CONDITIONS	ROD LENGTH	ROD ACTION	LINE SIZE	LURE WEIGHT	REEL SIZE
Light fresh and saltwater fish.	6 1/2'	LT	4-10 lbs.	1/8 to 3/8 oz. (Rod should have ultra-fast taper to handle a wide margin of lure weights. The light tip will cast light weights and the change to heavier line will allow the tip to handle the heavies.)	Medium Spin or Baitcasting
Light fresh and saltwater fish.	6 1/2'	MED/LT	8-15 lbs.	3/8 to 5/8 oz. (This in medium and fast taper is good for bass, walleyes and pike, bonefish, permit and small tarpon, using heavy jigs and bait or sinkers and bait.)	Medium Spin or Baitcasting
Medium saltwater and heavy freshwater fish.	5 1/2'	MED/UFT	10-20 lbs.	3/8 to 1 oz. (For rugged freshwater fishing as well as boat, bay and beach saltwater work, particularly trolling and heavy baiting. A rod built to stop fish such as snook from hanging in the mangroves or big striped bass.)	Medium Baitcasting
Casting and trolling heavy weights deep.	5 1/2'	V/HVY	17 to 50 lbs.	1 3/4 to 6 oz. (For muskellunge, lake trout, snook, tarpon and even dolphin, 'cuda and the like, if you don't try to kill too fast.)	Medium Saltwater
Trolling, jetty or heavy bottom fishing.	5 1/2'	V/HVY	17 to 50 lbs.	1 to 2 1/2 lbs. (Similar to above but preferred by bottom sinker bouncers as an all-purpose deep-trolling and big-fish rig up to school tuna.)	Medium Saltwater
Trolling, bottom fishing.	5 1/2'	LT	20 to 40 lbs.	2 1/2 to 4 oz. (Light bay and deep lake fishing with wire lines.)	Large Saltwater

(Legend: As in preceding recommended tackle table.)

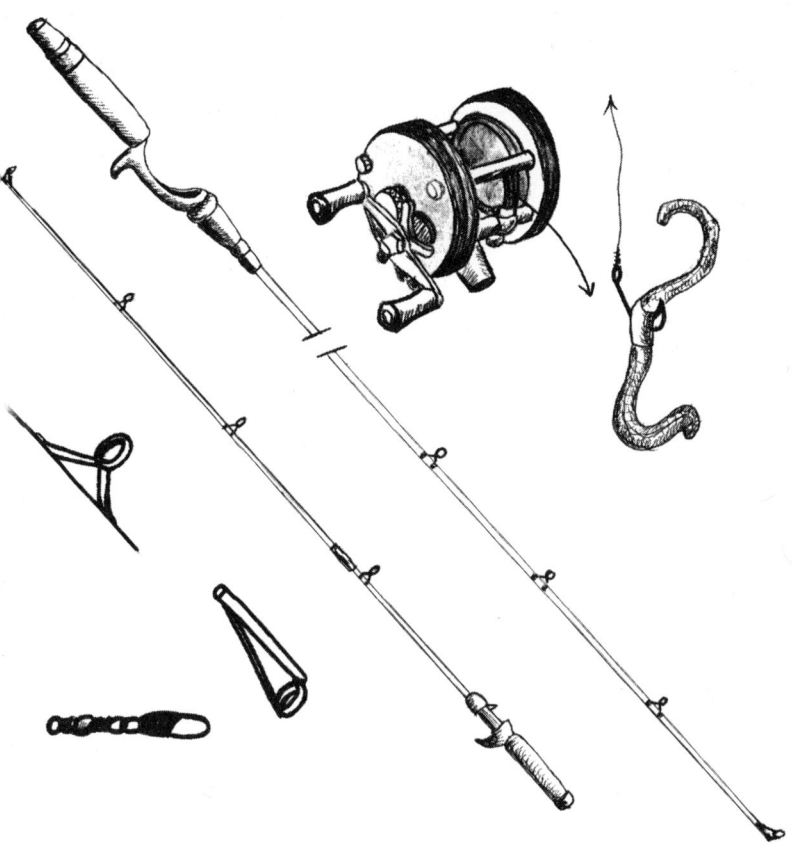

Typical offset-handled baitcasting rod and reel. The line feeds off the top of the reel spool. Rod guides are small since the line feeds directly through them rather than in coils as in spinning. Rods are two-piece, either the first section with the butt, or the butt, handle and first section in one piece, the tip being the second.

tackle for the particular bait fishing to be done locally. If planning an extended trip to an area where availability of tackle and terminal gear is bound to be scant or nonexistent, better bring along a large assortment and not excluding a good brand of lubricating oil. Reels should be taken apart at home so they can be put back together again after an "on the spot" cleaning at the fishing camp. Make sure rods are safely packed in tubular containers. Before putting the line on the reel, read and re-read the instructions carefully. Tackle dealers should demonstrate how, or quite literally do it for their customers on their line winders, quickly and efficiently. When assembling a rod, align the line leader guides *before* inserting the section into its ferrule joint. Do not twist or bend the rod while inserting or removing. If a line becomes snagged while fishing, do not strain the rod to get it free. Pull in the line directly; better to break a line and/or lose a rig than damage a rod.

REGULATION SALTWATER GEAR

Basic saltwater bait fishing rods, reels and terminal tackle are divided into overlapping categories: bottom fishing-trolling; general, all-purpose casting, and strictly distance casting rods. The rig can be either a conventional baitcasting or spinning type. Their function and requirements are similar and do the job.

For freshwater trolling and stillfishing, the general all-purpose medium-weight rigs will suffice for small fish species, but where greater weights, depths of water and heftier sinkers are used, heavier tackle is required. While it is possible for only one rod and reel to be used for all these purposes (par-

TACKLE TYPES

ticularly the spinning rod) it is better to fit the tackle closer to the task at hand.

The typical boat rod used for bottom bait fishing is not required to cast the bait any distance. Rod action need not be (nor should it be) too soft. In order to control bait at great depths, hook the fish on the first nibble and keep it from snagging bottom rocks and debris, it must respond to the slightest pull. When after big fish such as those found in extremely deep offshore waters and near shipwrecks, a stouter rod is used with a large-capacity reel and proportionately heavier line.

The casting rod is a different proposition. For the bait fisherman using a heavy sinker for distance, a fairly stiff-tipped rod is needed whether he be casting from a boat, jetty, point of rocks or the beach.

RIGGING AND HANDLING THE TACKLE

For boat fishing, trolling or bottom baiting for trout, bass and lake trout; in the bay for porgies, flounders, small grouper, southern sea trout, (possibly) striped bass, snook and similar species, take a boat rod of medium weight and length, attach a saltwater reel of correct line capacity filled with the proper line. Terminal rigging has been pre-selected for the type of fish and kind of bait.

The reel drag should be set at a point a few ounces under the line's breaking point so the line will pull off the reel before it breaks thus avoiding excessive strain on the rod. Practice with the combination by tying the line to something stationary. In this way the line's breaking limits can readily be discovered. Set the reel handle on anti-reverse so the handle will not spin on strike. For bottom fishing, merely drop the terminal tackle overboard and allow it to touch the bottom. Quickly reel in a foot or more, lifting the bait and sinkers off the bottom. It is best to hold the rod in both hands and be ready for a strike. One can also give some action to the bait by lifting the rod up and down rythmically. For trolling, set the rod in a rod holder if there is one on the boat, but watch it! Be careful not to allow fingers near the reel and never grab hold of the line on a strike. It can file right through to the bone if the fish is big.

HANDLING THE TACKLE FOR CASTING

Tackle set-up requires the line test again be taken into consideration. In addition, the baitcasting reel is adjusted for spool revolutions which ultimately control the line in casting. Some anglers prefer the spool to be "free" and fast; others like it controlled a bit to avoid backlash, especially when casting very light weights. The spincaster need not worry, for the line will come off the reel in direct relation to the pressure of the cast.

In order to effect the easiest and most effortless cast, select the tackle to fit the need of the moment. Actual techniques of casting and retrieving are described later after considering the various terminal tackle rigs most often used.

In fly fishing, most reels of the lighter variety do not have drag adjustments, but those that do can be set to accommodate a hard pull on the line by either fish or fisherman and will not allow a tangle due to overspin. The angler draws off the line by hand, so there is no required setting of the reel drag except as mentioned before in the case of big fighting fish circumstances, such as bonefish and Atlantic salmon—all played from the reel.

TACKLE TYPES

Since there are no controls on most fly reels, it is best to test the line strength. Attach the end of the leader to a stationary object and strain the rod and line to nearly the breaking point. Due to the spring of the long fly rod, much of the direct strain on the line is absorbed. It is surprising how much pressure can be applied before reaching the danger point for either rod or line.

TERMINAL TACKLE

Terminal tackle is the "business end" of the line, and combinations and variations of swivels, snaps, keels, sinkers and hooks are legion. There are, however, a few standard rigs that are designed for basic purposes. Improvising can be learned from experience. It is always advisable to consult the local fishermen, tackle dealers and guides as to correct arrangement and selection of terminal gear for the purposes and conditions that exist on the spot.

There are, for instance, several designs, wire thicknesses and sizes of hooks available. To own them all would be useless as well as confusing. Common sense will dictate the hook choice for the bait used and the size of the fish's mouth. Weights will be determined by the power of the rod for casting, current pull and, in the case of freshwater streams or ocean fishing, the prevailing currents or tides. The choice of two or three hooks, or a single hook rigged above or below the sinker is again determined by the conditions. The use of wire leaders as opposed to nylon monofilament is determined by the "boniness" and "toothiness" of the fish, and the ruggedness of the bottom to be covered. Swivels and snap swivels are used when necessary to keep the line from twisting on cast or when drifting in the current.

Note the accompanying illustrations of some standard rigs

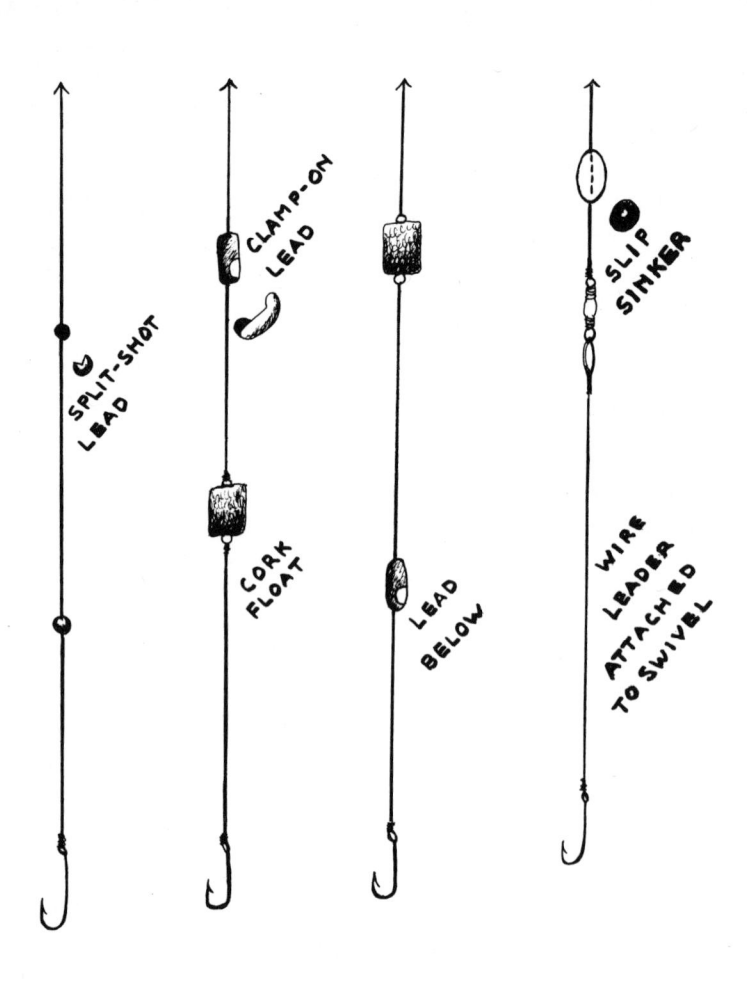

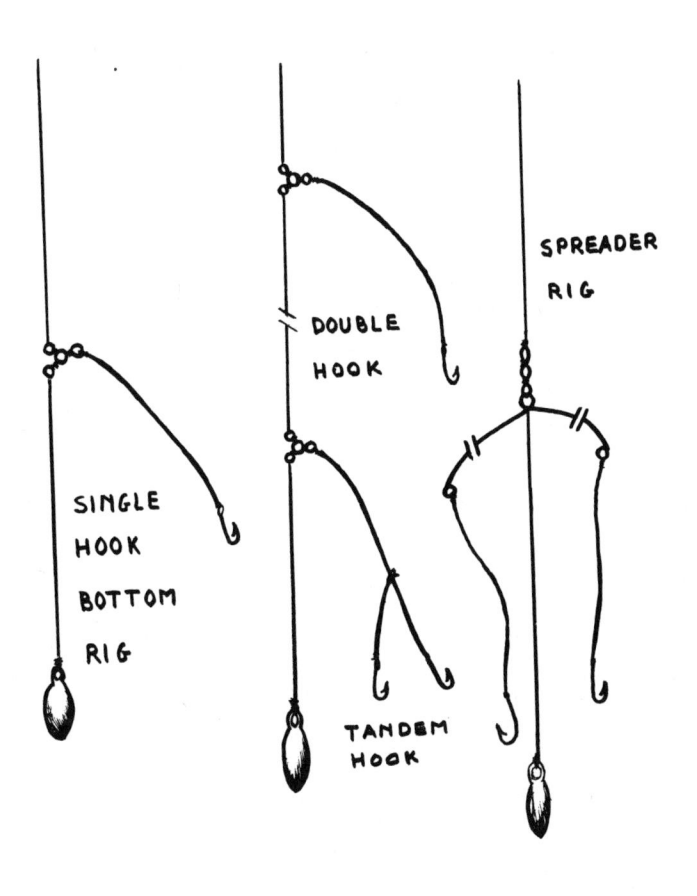

Some of the basic fresh and saltwater terminal rigs to become acquainted with. There are many variations of these.

and their general purpose. Go equipped for these situations. Have plenty of spare parts, because in bait fishing, especially bottom fishing, the fisherman becomes snagged quite often, necessitating the job of re-rigging.

KNOTS AND HOOKS

While there are more knots and hooks to be shown later, these few knots will suffice for almost any situation. Learn to tie them in the dark. It will be awkward at first and slow, but a little practice will perfect the technique and reduce the time needed to complete the knot securely. The hooks are labeled as to general types, and are among the most common and versatile. Actual bait hooking and hook choice is covered specifically in later chapters.

CASTING

The accompanying diagrams show casting methods for the three basic tackle types, flyfishing, spinning and baitcasting rods, and reels for bait fishing.

The bait fisherman does not have to cast as often; as accurately nor as far as the angler using artificial lures. The main point is to get the bait out as effortlessly as possible, being careful to make the cast so the bait will not be killed by snapping it in the air or slapping it down. Otherwise, the bait will likely be flipped off if the cast is too long or too short and off target.

Again, the fisherman should be armed with a balanced set of tackle—from rod choice right down to the balance of the combined weight of sinker and bait, plus proper leaders and other terminal tackle—and know how to cast the bait as accurately as possible.

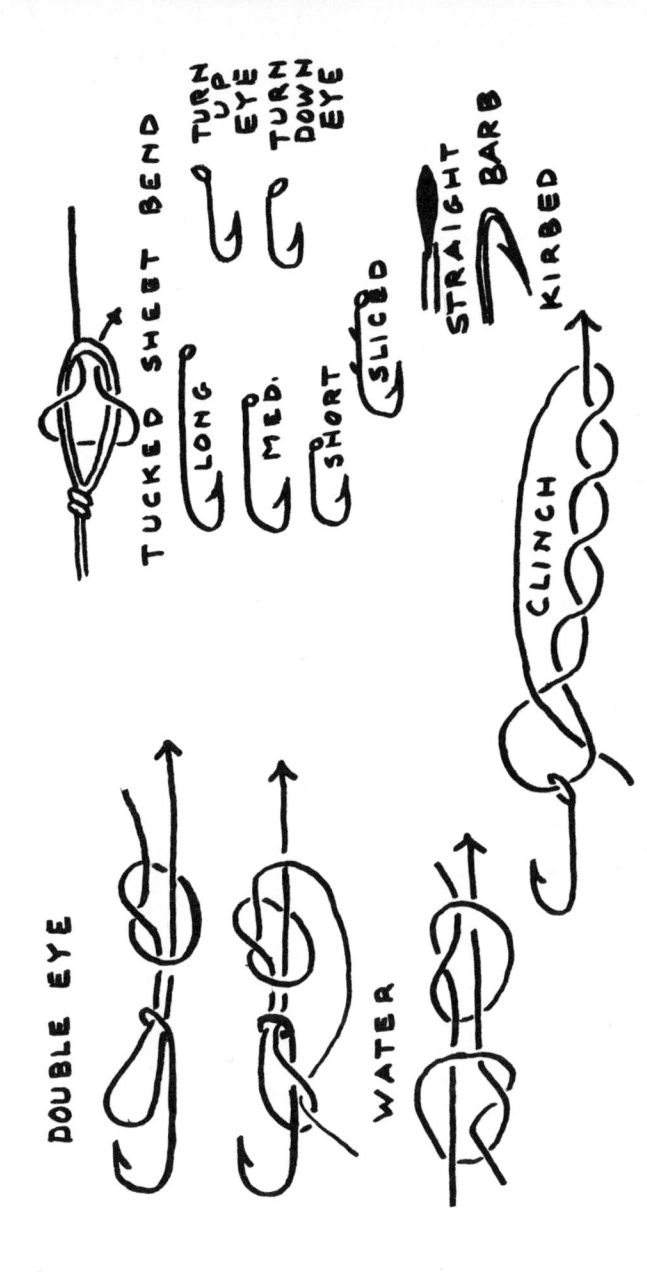

Some of the most common knots and hooks used in fishing.

In most descriptions of casting, the angler is advised to make the cast in a vertical swing. This is correct for casting lures and flies, but it is not advisable with bait, since the chance of snapping or flipping the bait off the hook is much greater than when using the common "side-winder" cast. This requires accurate timing in order to release the line at just the right instant in a circular swinging arc so that the bait and sinker go where desired. This type of casting takes time to master, but it is a necessity. The fisherman will also learn to vary his casting speed and power to suit the conditions, bait weights, and the distances desired.

GENERAL BAIT PRESENTATION AND RETRIEVES

While this subject will be more extensively covered in later chapters, some general hints are needed here for an immediate frame of reference.

When fishing a stream, river or tide run, the main idea is to put the bait where it will drift easily with the current and at the desired depth. It is therefore advisable to cast upstream, thereby permitting the longest drift of the bait before beginning its retrieve. Retrieving the bait will cause it to swing across an arc in the current below, and then return almost straight back to the boat or shoreline. If the water is shallow, hold the rod as high as possible to keep the bait up and drifting free of snags. Set the reel drag a little lighter than would be needed for fishing in still water. The strike of a fish plus the pull of a strong current can add up to quite a shock to tackle. After the strike, tighten up the drag to prevent the fish from running too far.

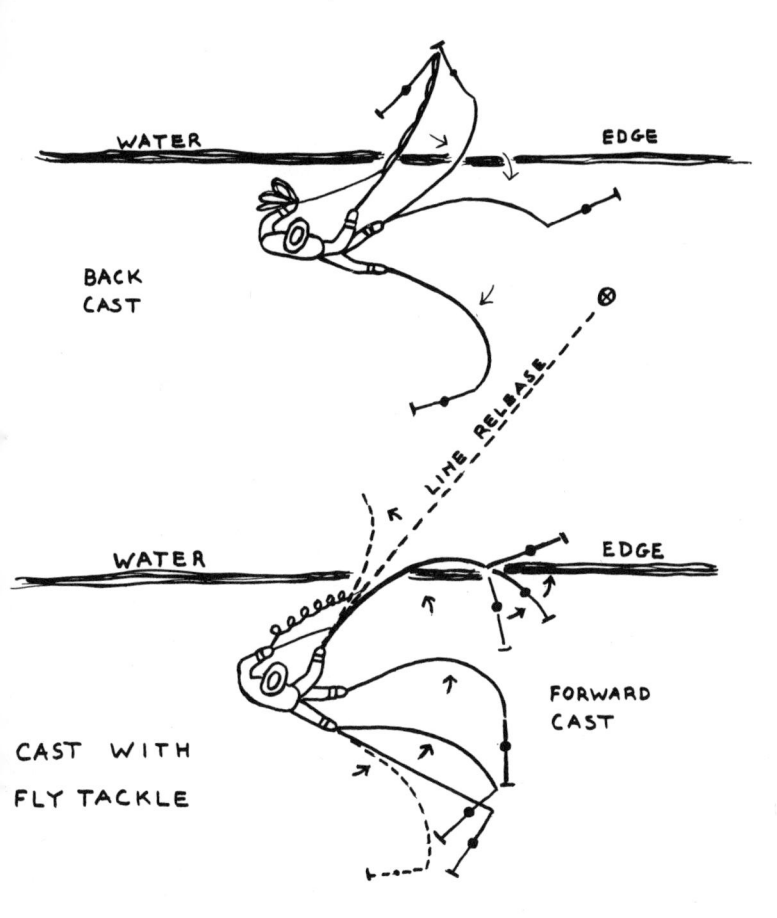

Baitcasting with the fly rod. In many instances it is necessary to cast with a side swing rather than to cast with a vertical movement lest the bait be jerked off the hook. This is trickier casting, especially when accuracy is at stake, and it necessitates learning the exactly correct split-second for line release.

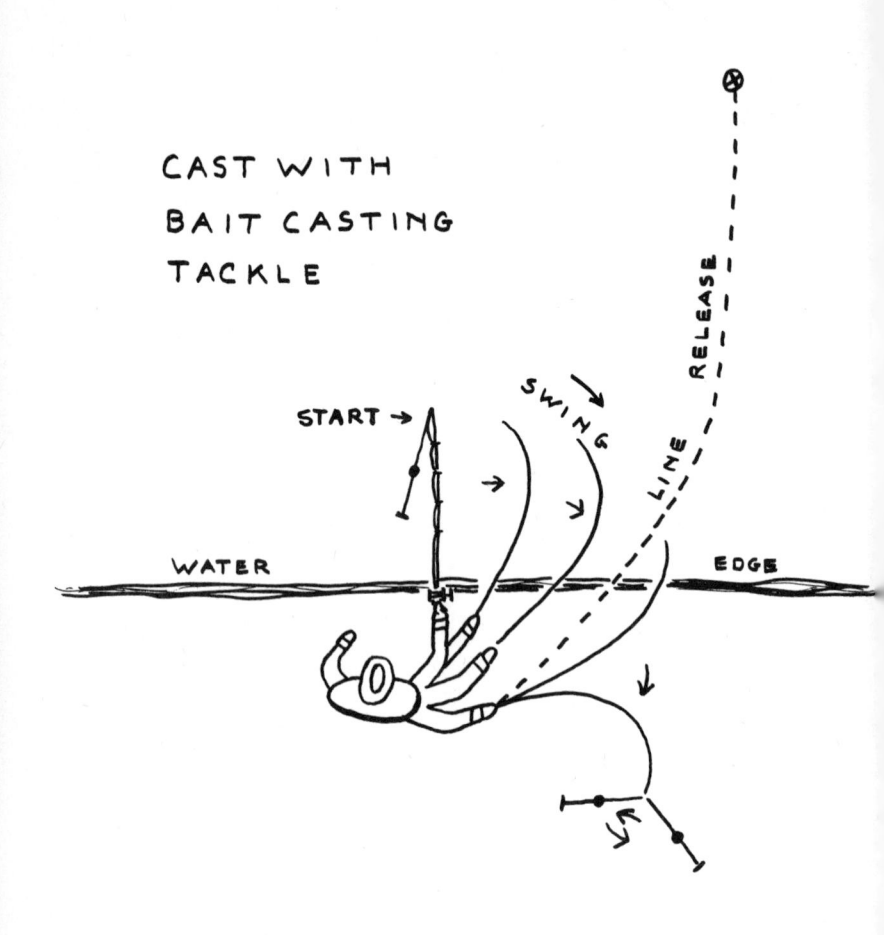

How to cast using baitcasting tackle.

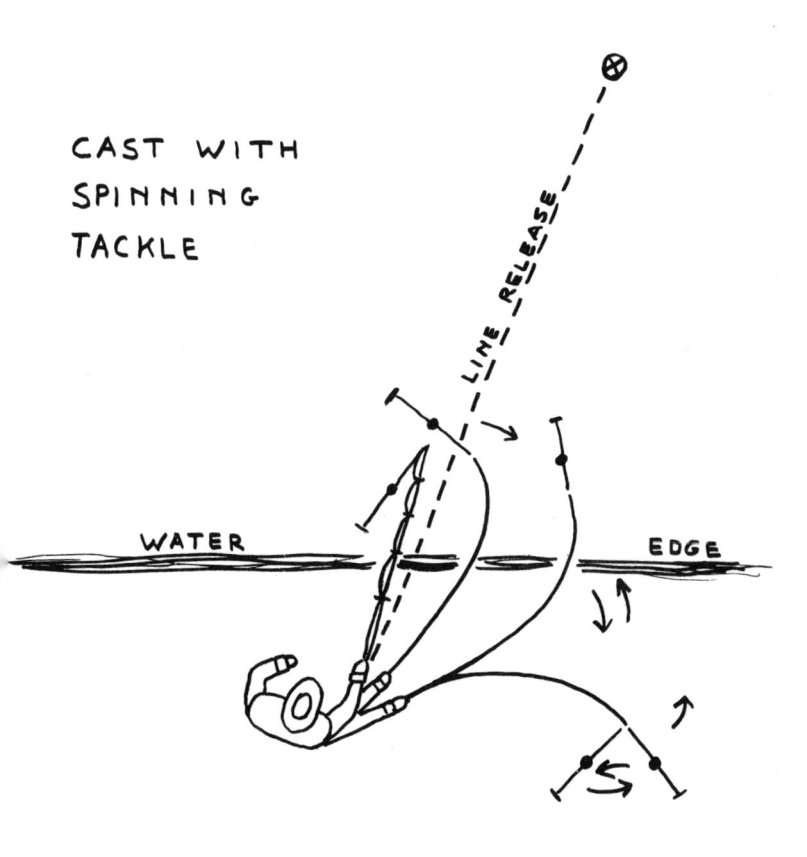

Casting with spinning tackle. When using such tackle in fishing from a stream bank, guard against overcasting and possibly wrapping your bait around tree branches protruding from the opposite side.

For quiet-water fishing, cast the bait to a certain spot, let it sink and rest there for a while, then very slowly reel it in, changing its position and giving it just enough action to make it more appealing to the fish. While most bait fishing is done close to the bottom, there are times when the bait is kept fairly near the surface. Often this way it is fished in combination with a large floating bobber. This is called "popper fishing" where retrieving with action on the bait is advised. This is an effective method for sea trout and many other gamesters, particularly if they are following schools of baitfish.

Don't neglect to alter terminal tackle when conditions warrant. Quite often, with a change of tide, variance of stream speed or water depth, it is advisable to adjust the depth to which the bait will sink. This can be done by either using a lighter sinker or a longer or shorter line from the bobber. Bait depth can also be altered by the speed of the retrieve after the cast or, when trolling, by varying the speed of the boat. The trick is to blend these variations into the conditions at hand.

Inspect live bait often and replace it whenever it appears to be getting "tired."

When well versed at building terminal rigs and casting, the fisherman can begin to fish two rods at the same time. This is practical even though he may have to handle the boat and motor at the same time.

Trolling is a great deal simpler than casting and, if done properly, can net a catch worth boasting about. Moving around the lake or bay, a lot of "ground" can be covered in a short time. Get to know the underwater contours, deep holes and drop-offs and work over them, back and forth. In the lakes, especially during the hot weather, try and locate the

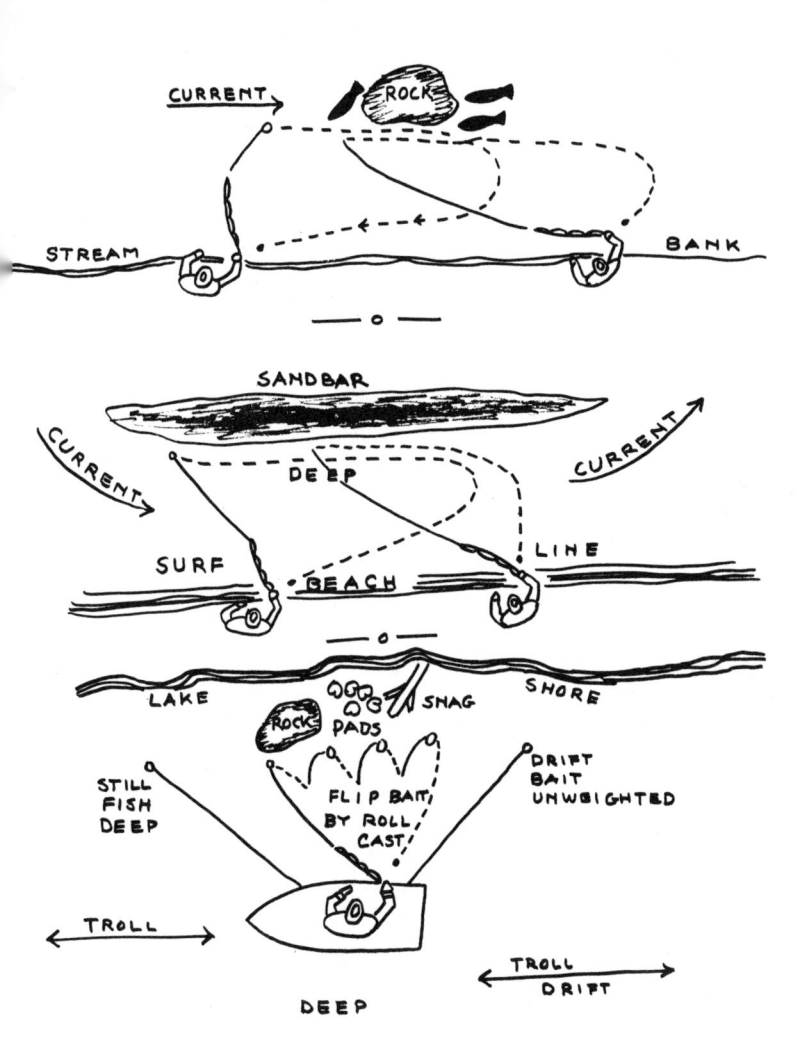

Examples of general bait presentation and retrieve in fresh and saltwater fishing.

deepest holes. Fish will be settling there. Spring holes are another fishing hot spot. Use a thermometer to locate the temperature margin between 60 and 70 degrees Fahrenheit, and "plumb" for depth by dropping a weighted line to the bottom. The use of a geodetic map is recommended for an unfamiliar lake, since one quick look at it will indicate where to fish—field knowledge that is every bit as important as knowing *how* to fish.

STRIKING, PLAYING, LANDING

These three operations require of the fisherman a knowledge of exactly what he and his tackle can accomplish. If he has experimented as recommended earlier and knows the extremes of his gear and its limitations, he can then strike, play and land his fish with the rising confidence that accompanies experience. Now the pressure bend of the rod offsets the action of the fish and varies with the rod's length, degree of bend exerted and inherent strength. The line must be similarly considered. Too much strain will break it or the terminal leader. Hooks can pull out or snap from "horsing" the fish or trying to kill a fish too soon rather than playing it. Learn to give the fish a sporting chance. Don't try to land it in too quickly, except in the case of very soft-mouthed fish. Actually, fish weight has little to do with the degree of pull they can exert. A five-pound bonefish, for example, can run out under full rod pressure to a length of fifty yards, while a trout of identical weight will not run fifty feet. An Atlantic salmon can jump twenty times in a single minute while a carp three times heavier will merely tug the line around in a circle.

TACKLE TYPES

In striking, playing and landing, learn to handle the changes between rod spring pressure and line control; either manual, as in the case of fly fishing tackle, or by the adjustable drag on the reel.

Never try to strike or play a fish with the rod pointed directly toward the fish. The direct pull on the line, especially if the strike or action is heavy and in fast moving water, will break the line or leader and possibly pull the hook loose. On strike, immediately raise the rod tip or bring it back horizontally so that the entire length of the rod acts as the cushion.

Maintain an even pressure spring by retrieving or releasing line when the fish demands it. If one is not careful and does not maintain this balance, the fish will overstrain. On the other hand, understraining allows a slack or loose line to develop. Once this pressure between fisherman and fish is lacking, the hook can easily pull loose, drop out of the fish's mouth or, if the fish is active, he can and will jump and thrash his head back and forth in efforts to get rid of the hook.

Most fish will come in long before their fight is exhausted. Then they'll scare and explode at close hand in an effort to escape. Be prepared for this by careful line control and applied rod pressure. Be prepared to vary both in a split second.

When the fish is considered ready for the net, submerge the hoop. Do not try and play tennis with the fish. Don't try to net the fish directly; instead, submerge the net and guide the fish into it, not relaxing line control or rod pressure until it is safely inside the hoop. In hand-landing fish into a boat, it is better not to lift the fish by the rod, especially in the case of a heavy fish and a light line. Slip a hand down the leader and grasp either the leader or the fish's gill and hoist it

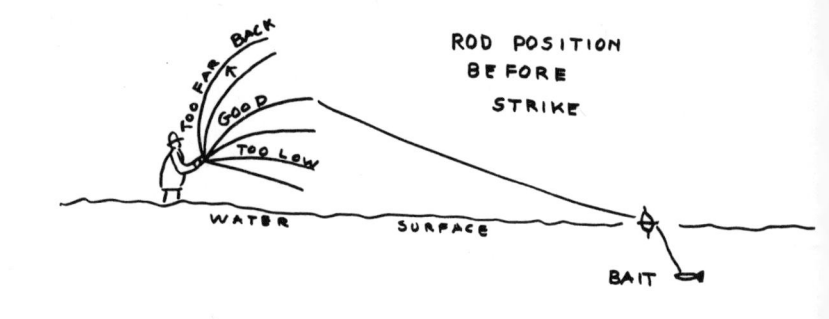

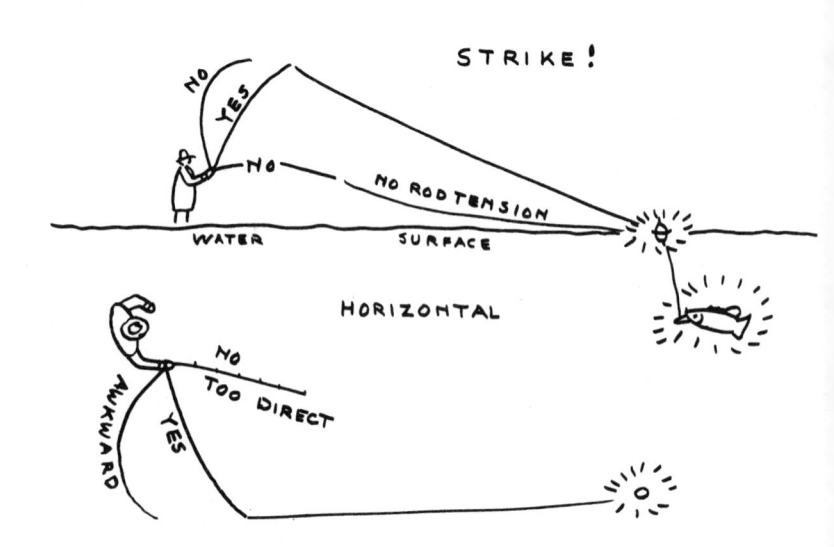

Special rod handling and line control are required when striking and playing a fish as shown in these diagrams. The rule is use the rod as a cushion.

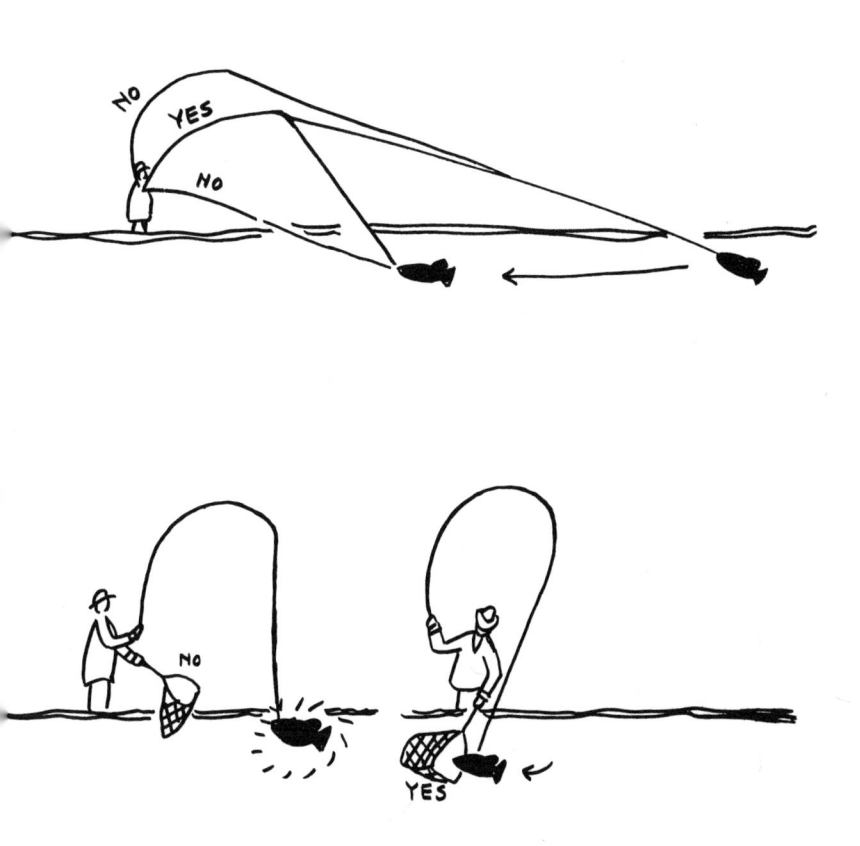

Again, use the rod as a cushion. Do the same when landing the fish.

aboard. In the case of large saltwater game fish or spiny coarse fish, the use of a gaff is advised. Then kill the fish before trying to unhook it. Severe cuts can be gotten from scales and spiney fins or one can even be bitten by fish that are still thrashing while the fisherman is fumbling with their bridge-work!

4
Fish of Most Interest to Sportsmen

THE NORTHERN HEMISPHERE is blessed with hundreds of beautiful, hard-fighting, good-eating species of sport and food fish. To appreciate this great heritage, conservation should be an ethic vital to every sport and recreational fisherman.

FRESHWATER SPECIES

The popularity of freshwater fishing is certainly not confined to those living only in inland states. As a matter of fact, four of the ten states listed several years ago as having the largest number of fishing license sales were states where saltwater fishing was also available. So let's look at six categories of freshwater species that offer so much fishing fun to so many anglers.

The Trouts

Six major species of trout inhabit the brooks, streams and lakes of our northern countryside and Canada. The brook trout, actually a char (Salvelinus fontinalis), once native of New England, has become widely distributed across the map. One-half to two-pounders make a good meal and a record-breaker may even range to five pounds.

The rainbow (Salmo gairdneri), cutthroat (Salmo clarki), and steelhead (sea-run rainbow) are essentially West Coast and West-of-the-Mississippi species. The rainbow has been introduced into Eastern waters and is now considered "native." Good catches range from five to twenty-five pounds.

The brown trout (Salmo trutta) is an import from Europe and, since 1880, a naturalized citizen, ranging in size from one to twenty-five pounds and more.

All these species feed on aquatic stream and lake insects, minnows and blow-ins and are taken in legal season by a variety of tackle.

The lake trout (Salvelinus namaycush), similar to the brook trout, is somewhat larger and is found mainly in northern lakes.

Pacific Salmons

All of these salmon, the coho (Oncorhynchus kisutch), the chinook (Oncorhynchus tshawytscha) and the sockeye (Onchorhynchus nerka), are ocean inhabitants of the Pacific

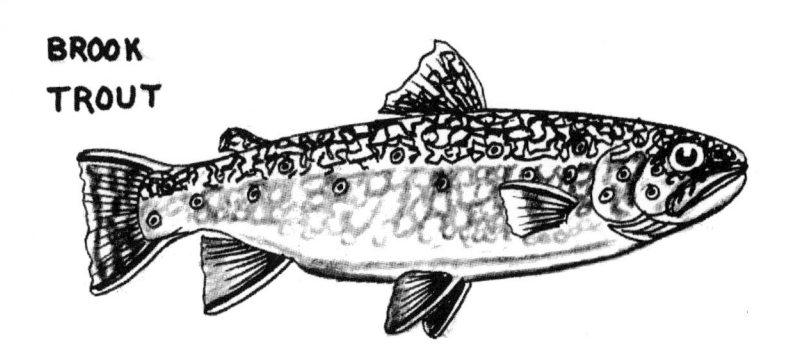

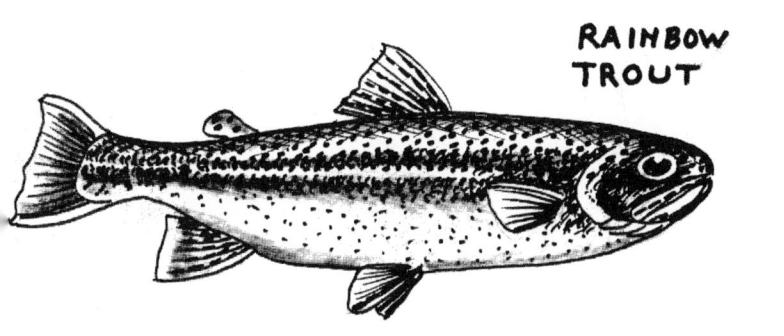

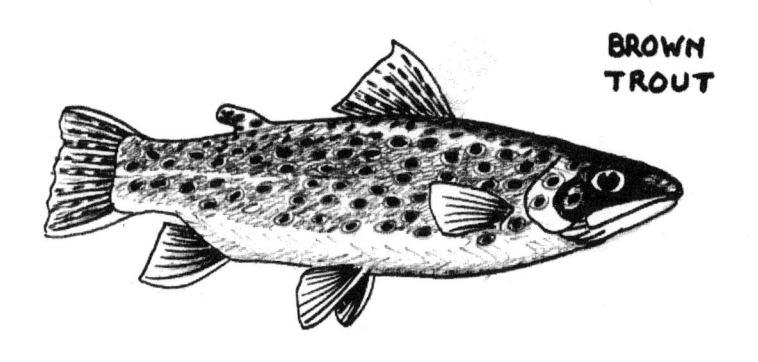

BROOK TROUT

RAINBOW TROUT

BROWN TROUT

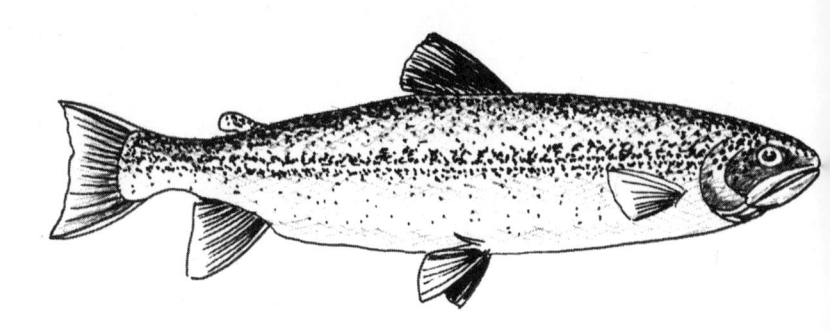

PACIFIC SALMON (type)

Northwest and Alaska; ascending the rivers and streams to spawn. While in salt water, they are trolled and cast for in the bays as they approach the spawning rivers. Baitfish are trolled, usually in combination with spoons and spinners to attract them. Bait fishing is not done, however, once these fish are in the true stream. Other salmon, the Atlantic and the landlocked of northeastern waters, are rarely taken on bait, and fly-fishing-only is the rule for Atlantics. Powerful jumpers and long runners, they offer kingly sport in their ten to fifty-pound range. Spinning gear and baitcasting tackle are used and trolling is of the shallow variety. The salmon is a best-rated food fish.

Freshwater Basses

Two common species are represented in the large bass family in our fresh waters. They are the largemouth bass (Micropterus salmoides), and the smallmouth bass (Micropterus dolomieui). They are similar in shape and markings, though

FISH OF MOST INTEREST TO SPORTSMEN

LARGEMOUTH BASS

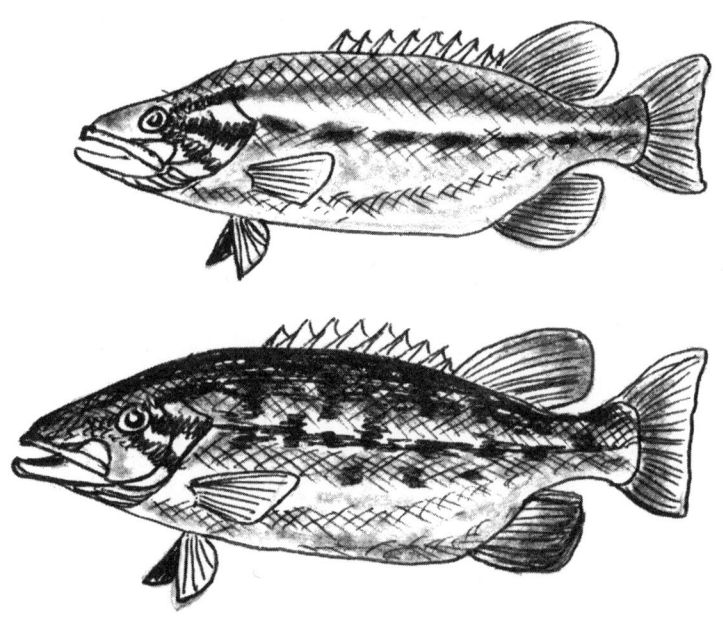

SMALLMOUTH BASS

the smallmouth is a bit slimmer and more bronze. The relative position of the upper jaw and the eye help to identify the differences of each species.

A good catch of largemouths would range from three to ten pounds; larger in the Deep South; the smallmouth would be big at six pounds. Primarily lake and slow stream species, they are also found in faster rivers and brooks that enter into or empty from large lakes and impoundments. Their basic food is anything that moves, from mice to frogs, small birds to minnows and aquatic insects. They are taken on fly, spin and baitcasting tackle.

Northern Pike, Muskellunge and Walleye Pike

These two species, the northern pike (Esox lucius), and the muskellunge (Esox masquingy) are our two largest species of game fish. They are quite similar in shape, varying in skin markings and head details. They are found only in the more northern states and Canada, and have not been introduced as widely as the trouts and basses.

Their food is similar to the basses, but due to their larger size, they eat larger minnows, other game and food fish, aquatic insects, birds, mice and frogs. These are fierce fighters and heavy tackle is needed. Trolling is the most popular method and in the summertime, deep trolling is what gets them. A big pike will range from fifteen to twenty-five pounds and a prize musky will go to forty pounds.

The walleye pike (Stizostedion vitreum vitrium), looks like a combination of a pike and a perch. The specie is a trifle smaller than the northern pike and the muskellunge and not a strong battler. The walleye usually ranges from five to ten pounds, but many are caught each summer weighing far more.

The walleye is prized as a tasty food fish.

The chain pickerel (Esox niger), found in lakes and slow rivers is another smaller version of the pike, usually ranging from two to five pounds, although many are taken well over these weights. The pickerel is a fierce fighter on light tackle.

NORTHERN PIKE

MUSKELLUNGE

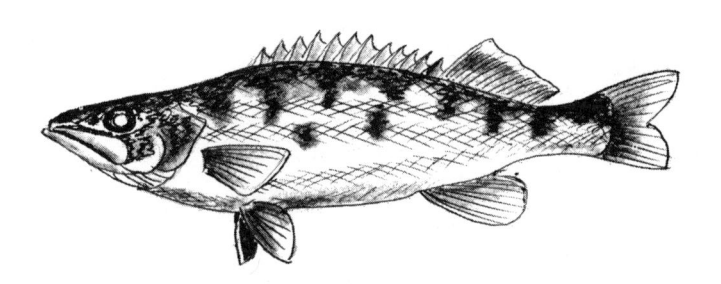

WALLEYE PIKE

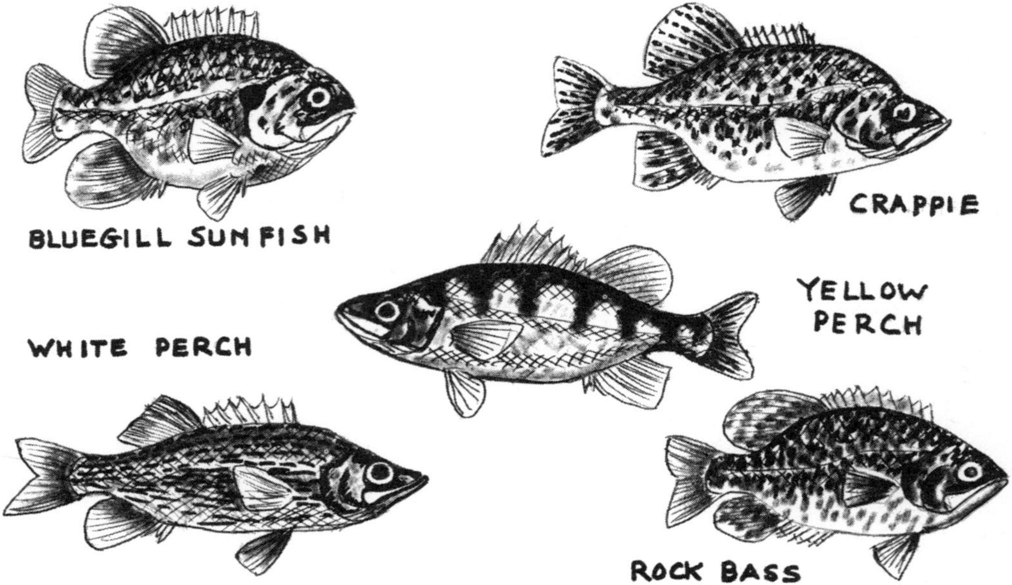

BLUEGILL SUNFISH
CRAPPIE
YELLOW PERCH
WHITE PERCH
ROCK BASS

FISH OF MOST INTEREST TO SPORTSMEN

General Panfish

In the perch family, yellow (Perca flavescens), and white (Roccus americanus); the crappie family, white (Pomoxis annularis), and black (Pomoxis nigromaculatus) are our most common species. The sunfish family includes the bluegill sunfish (Lepomis macrochirus) and the several varieties of smaller species. All are found in most waters, particularly through the Central United States and the Southland. They are small, plentiful and full of fight for their size. They are energetic feeders, particularly on surface baits. Their diet consist of aquatic and blow-in insects and small minnows. Gear of the ultra-light category is best used to enjoy these splashing, spunky little fighters. They range in size from one-half pound to three pounds.

Other Panfish

Included in this category, for convenience and brevity, are several species which are only "unofficially" considered game fish, since they do offer fun on light tackle. The catfish family is a large one with the blue (Ictalurus melas), and the channel (Ictalurus punctatus) the principal and larger cats. The carp (Cyprinus carpio) belongs to the "goldfish" family. The suckers, another large family, are represented by several species, the lake chubsucker (Erimyzon sucetta) having the widest distribution. They are all bottom feeders and their diet ranges from aquatic vegetation and man-made concoctions of smelly baits, fish or insects, as in the case of the catfish. The channel catfish grows to forty pounds in the large rivers and carp will weigh from four to forty pounds. Suckers and fallfish in their myriad variations range up to two or three pounds. All can be taken on light to medium freshwater tackle and appropriate baits.

SUCKER

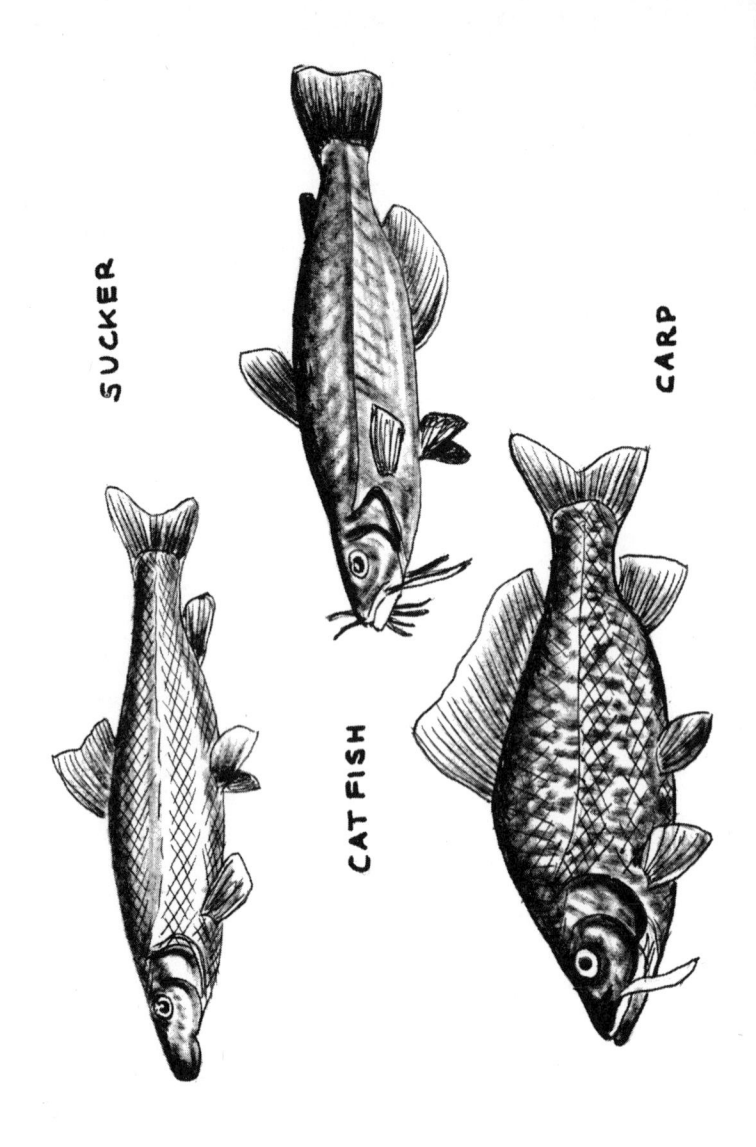

CAT FISH

CARP

FISH OF MOST INTEREST TO SPORTSMEN

SALTWATER SPECIES

Striped, Channel Bass and Seabass

Three of the most popular of the large saltwater bass family, the striped bass (Roccus saxatilis), channel bass (Sciaenops ocellatus) and sea bass of many species are found on both coasts. The striped bass were introduced to the State of Oregon from the East. They range along the shore; not being found in the open ocean in company with marlins and tunas. They are semi-andronomous, often spawning in the brackish waters of inlets and river outlets that afford easy escape from saltwater. Their food consists of the shellfish, aquatic life of all kinds including shrimp, school baitfish, shellfish, crabs and sea worms. They are fished (depending on seasonal conditions) from the bottom to the top with the exception of the sea bass which remain in deep waters most of the year. Trolling and casting is done along the shore for stripers and channel bass, but bottom fishing is recommended for the numerous species of sea bass.

They range in weight from three to fifty pounds. California black sea bass (Stereolepis) range up to two hundred pounds.

Pollock, Cod and Bluefish

These three species are grouped here for the purposes of regional and similar fishing considerations rather than by category. They are limited in range to the East Coast, the pollock (Pollachius virens) and cod (Gadus callarias) ranging from Newfoundland to Cape Cod; the bluefish (Pomatomus saltratrix) ranging from Cape Cod to Florida. The pollock is essentially a bottom fish similar to the cod, but yet unlike the

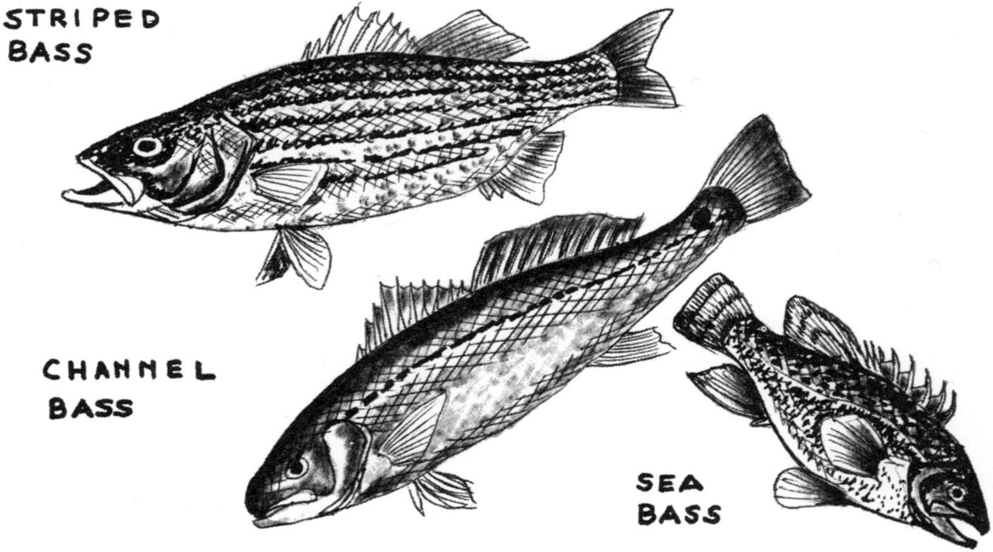

STRIPED BASS
CHANNEL BASS
SEA BASS

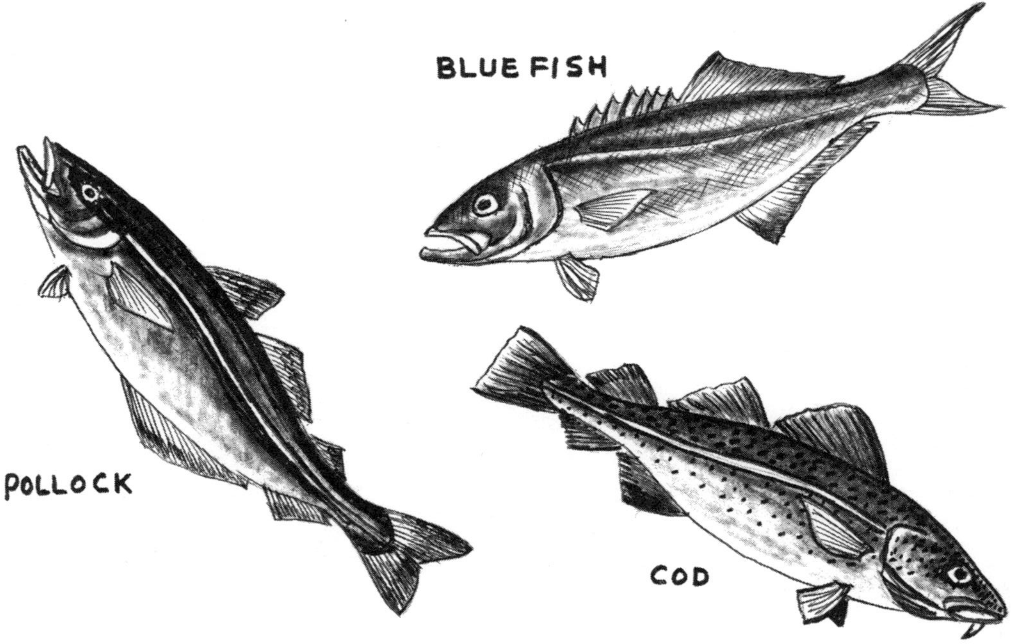
BLUE FISH
POLLOCK
COD

cod, it is found in the spring and fall along the beaches and points of land, feeding on roving schools of baitfish in company with the bluefish and striped bass. The cod remains out in the deep ocean and is a favorite of partyboat anglers and those who like to bounce their sinkers on the bottom. Striped bass and bluefish afford much sport to anglers fishing from the beach, jetties and points of land. They usually cast or troll for them mostly in the tide rips, inlets and river mouths. All manner of light to heavy tackle is used and bait consists of crustaceans, shrimp, squid, sand or sea worms and school baitfish common at the scene. Strong fighters, these denizens of the briny blue range in size from three to forty pounds.

Saltwater Panfish, Flounders, Porgies, etc.

The *et cetera* includes skates and a half-hundred species of bottom fish found in bays, inlets, beaches, mudflats and rocky bottoms, inshore and offshore. The Atlantic halibut is a large flounder or fluke weighing up to four hundred pounds. There are simply too many of these species to cover in a single book, the summer flounder (Paralichthys dentatus) and the porgie, known as the scaup (Stenotomus chrysops) and the sheepshead (Archosargus probatocephalus) being the most common. Variations of all are found on both coasts, being caught frequently by trolling, but mostly by bottom fishing. The flounders inhabit sandy and mud bottoms, while the porgies are found in sandy and rocky bottoms and around old wrecks. Flounders range in weight from one to four pounds; the porgies up to twenty pounds. Food consists of crustaceans, crabs, worms, and small fish. Light to medium tackle is used, except in cases of giant halibut.

PORGIE

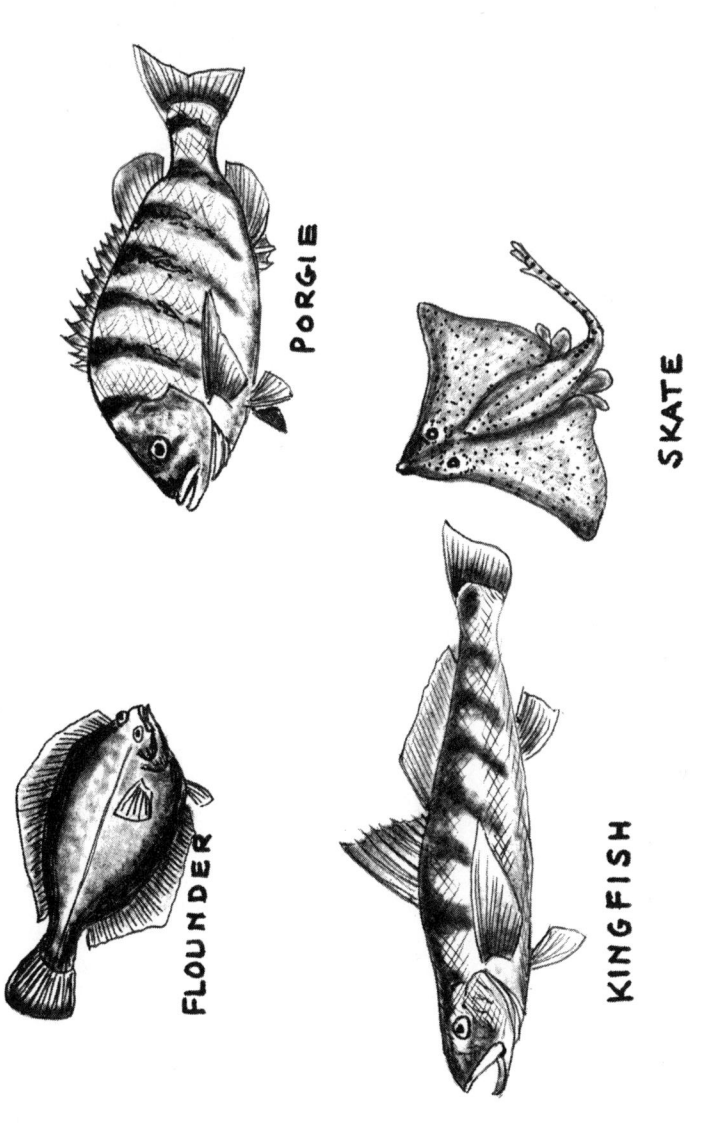

SKATE

FLOUNDER

KINGFISH

WEAKFISH

Weakfish and Sea Trout

These two species are quite similar in markings, size and shape. They feed on crustaceans, small baitfish, sea worms, shrimp and cut bait. The common weakfish of northern waters (Cynoscion regalis) ranges from Cape Cod to Maryland, while the spotted sea trout or weakfish (Cynoscion nebulosus) ranges to Florida and around the Gulf Coast into Texas and Mexico. Both are considered tops in food value and offer sport in the inshore estuaries, inlets, bays, and inland waterways. They are found in brackish waters. They are similar in shape to the freshwater trout with the exception of the extended dorsal fin. They are sporty, even when small, if fished on light tackle and are favorites with bridge, jetty, beach and small boat anglers. Light saltwater and light freshwater tackle can be used. Weakfish range in size from one to five pounds and the spotted sea trout can go as high as ten pounds or better.

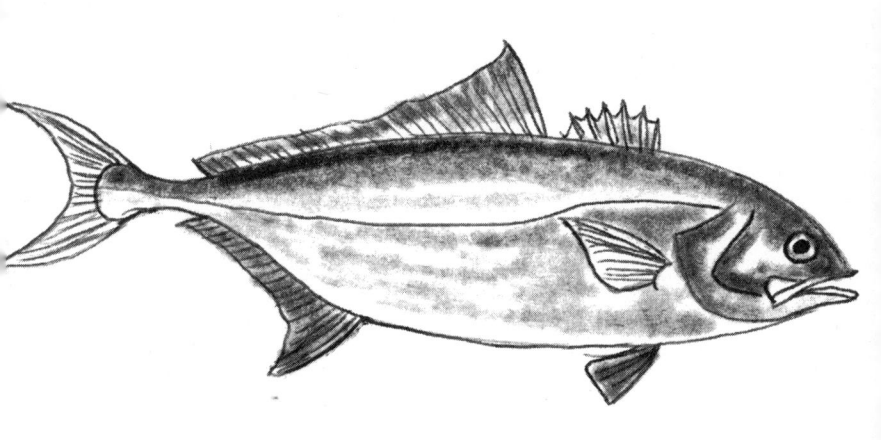

AMBERJACK

POMPANO

Pompano, Jacks, Permit and Amberjack

This family of fish has many species, only the most popular of which are included here. The common pompano (Trachinotus carolinus) along with the round and long fin are found from Cape Hattaras to the entire range of outer islands; Cuba and around the Florida peninsula along the Gulf Coast. Pompano bait includes cut fish, sand fleas plus numerous crustaceans, crabs and shrimp. The common jack (Caranx hippos) along with the horse-eye, blue runner and yellow are similar in habitat and diet. They range in weight from five to ten pounds. The great amberjack (Seriola zonata) is found in deep water from New Jersey to the West Indies and specimens range to over one-hundred pounds. Warm waters, off-shore flats, reefs and wrecks are its habitat. Big gear is needed here to keep this one from fouling a fishing line on the bottom.

Snook and Tarpon

These two gamesters will truly test tackle and angling skill. Found from Georgia to the Florida peninsula and along the Gulf Coast to Mexico, they offer sport to millions of light and medium-tackle anglers. The snook (Centropomus undecimalis) resembles the cod in shape but not in action. Found near and in inshore waters, bays, inlets, protected waterways and especially among the mangroves. Both the snook and the tarpon (Tarpon atlanticus) feed on shrimp, mullet and other baitfish. Snook run to thirty pounds and while tarpon run smaller in the rivers and estuaries, they're caught as big as one hundred and fifty pounds to as high as two hundred pounds. Taken by trolling, stillfishing and casting,

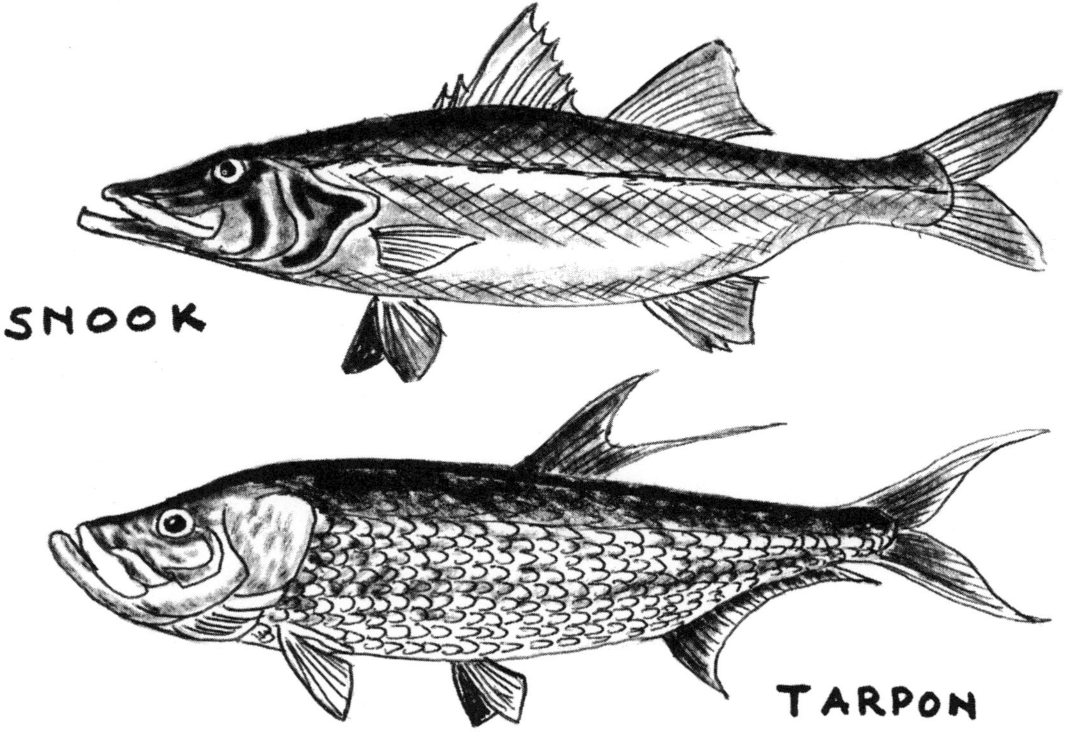
SNOOK
TARPON

both species are worth the effort and will provoke tall tale telling. Tarpon are not good table fare, but snook are cookbook classics.

Boston, Spanish and King Mackerel

Boston mackerel (Scomber scombrus) range from Newfoundland to Cape Hattaras and are prized as a food fish but considered small as gamesters go, reaching only four pounds. The Spanish mackerel (Scomberomorus maculatus) grows twice the size and inhabits warmer waters, as in the tropics. Both are school fish and the angler can catch a bucketfull in a few minutes. Bits of fish flesh, shrimp or beach minnows are best baits. Small freshwater tackle, even fly rods, are used.

The king mackerel (Scomberomorus cavalla) is much larger and taken regularly up to one hundred pounds. At times they are found inshore accompanied by the Spanish mackerel, but more frequently they are in offshore waters with dolphin and sailfish. Big tackle needed here and baits are those used for general big game fish: mackerel, bonefish, mullet.

Bonefish, Ladyfish

The bonefish (Albula vulpes) is the fastest running fish when hooked and held. Taken in the shallows of South Florida, the Bahamas and outer islands, the hooked fish has only one way to go and that's to the wide open sea, where it heads with alarming power and speed. Heavy fly tackle, spinning gear and light-tipped rods and heavy-duty baitcasting reels with at least one hundred yards of backing are needed. The bait can be conch, shrimp, crabs or bits of fish depending on the circumstances. These fish weigh from six to nine pounds.

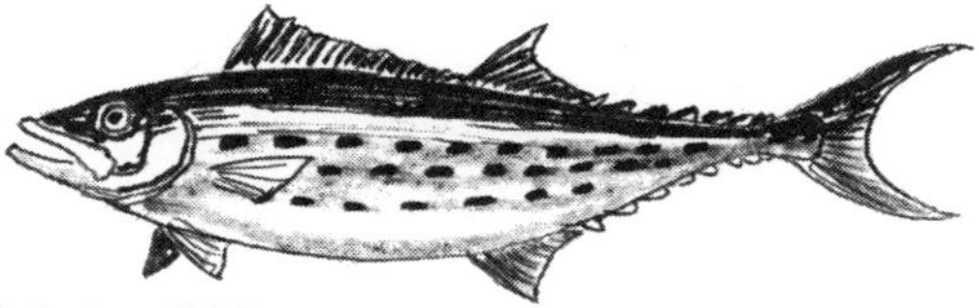

SPANISH MACKEREL

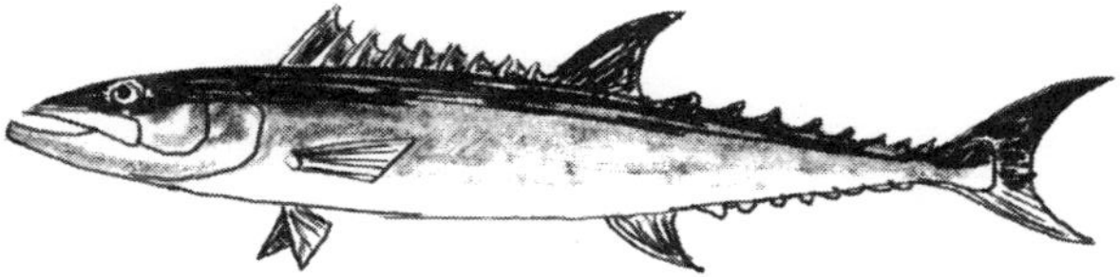

KING MACKEREL

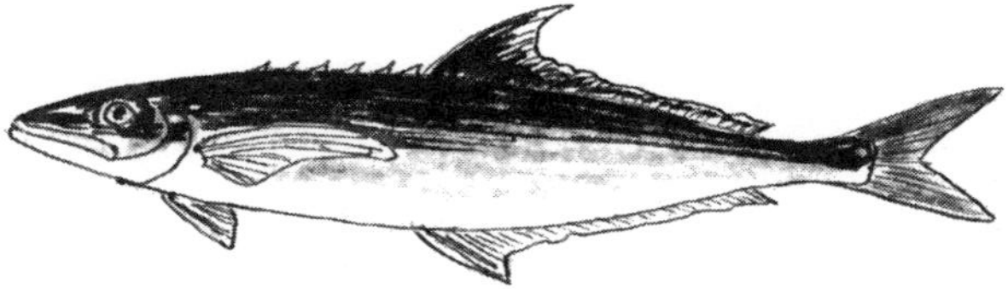

COBIA

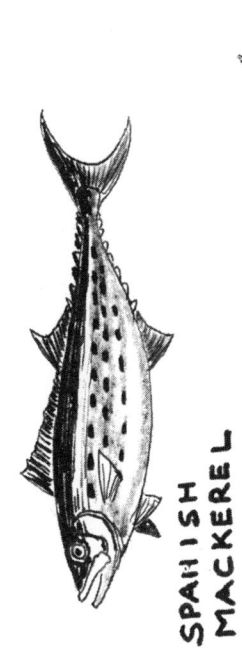

The ladyfish (Elops saurus) is similar in appearance though not as fast as the bonefish. It's found in similar circumstances when in on the broad flats from the deep to feed; weighs up to ten pounds.

BONEFISH

LADYFISH

FISH OF MOST INTEREST TO SPORTSMEN

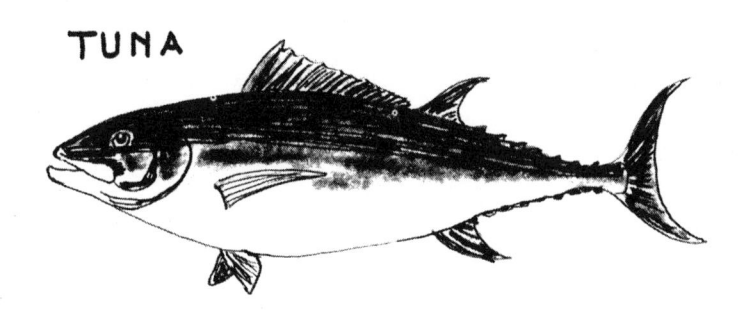

TUNA

Tunas, Albacore and Bonito

This is a big family with fish widely ranging in size from ten to seven hundred pounds. The big game angler knows the bluefin tuna (Thunnus thynus) on sight due to its immense size. It's found near Cuba, Newfoundland and the Atlantic Coast. The blackfin (Parathunnus thynnus) and California's yellowfin (Neothunnus macropterus) run from ten, fifty to one hundred pounds or more. There are several small, localized species of tuna also taken by offshore big game anglers. Big rigs, here, fighting chairs and well-equipped cruisers are necessary for the best sport. Bait is generally trolled squid, menhaden, herring, bonefish or mackerel. Fishing grounds are generally well offshore and the species are not infrequently accompanied by marlin, wahoo and dolphin.

Marlin (Black, White, Striped, Blue)

Commonly referred to as "billfish" because of the long sword preceding it by one-third its length, the marlin is taken well off shore from Cape Cod to South America—in fact, the marlin is taken in most open ocean waters of the world in one species or the other. The white marlin (the smallest) ranges in weight from sixty to eighty pounds, while the black marlin tips the scales at well over five hundred pounds. Big game tackle, fighting chair and outrigger fishing cruisers capable of long offshore trips are required. Baits used are bonefish, bluefish, mackerel, ladyfish, mullet and the like. Baits are trolled from outriggers and the angler sits patiently until the skipper's call pierces the dull grinding of the boat engine: "Marlin, marlin sighted on port bow . . ."

Sharks

There are numerous members of the shark family, but only five will be considered here—these are the big ones whose weight and sporting characteristics make them outstanding. The mako (Isurus oxyrhynchus); the white (Carcharodon carcharias); the porkbeagle (Lamma basus); the thresher (Alpias vulpins) and the tiger (Galeocerdo cuvier) all have several qualities in common: heavy weight, up to six hundred pounds; insatiable appetites for meat, animal blood and dead fish of any size and description; nasty tempers; terrible teeth and seemingly unbeatable, unending endurance under pressure from the biggest sporting tackle made.

In recent years, more anglers have taken to the specific sport of shark fishing and hence outfitting their boats for real trouble. Gallons of animal blood are poured over the side to form a blood slick on the ocean to attract them. Once hooked, sharks can strain and drain an angler for many hours.

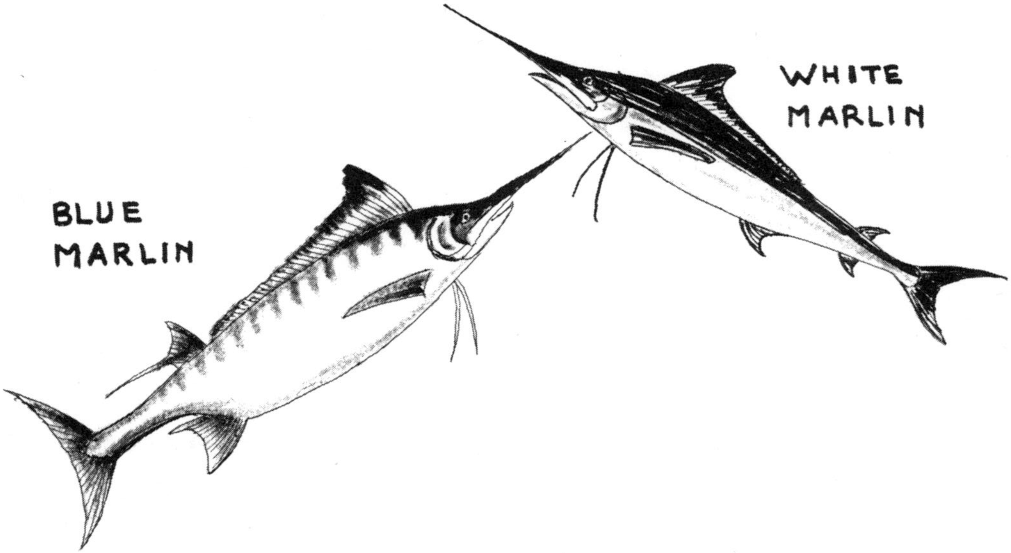

BLUE
MARLIN
WHITE
MARLIN

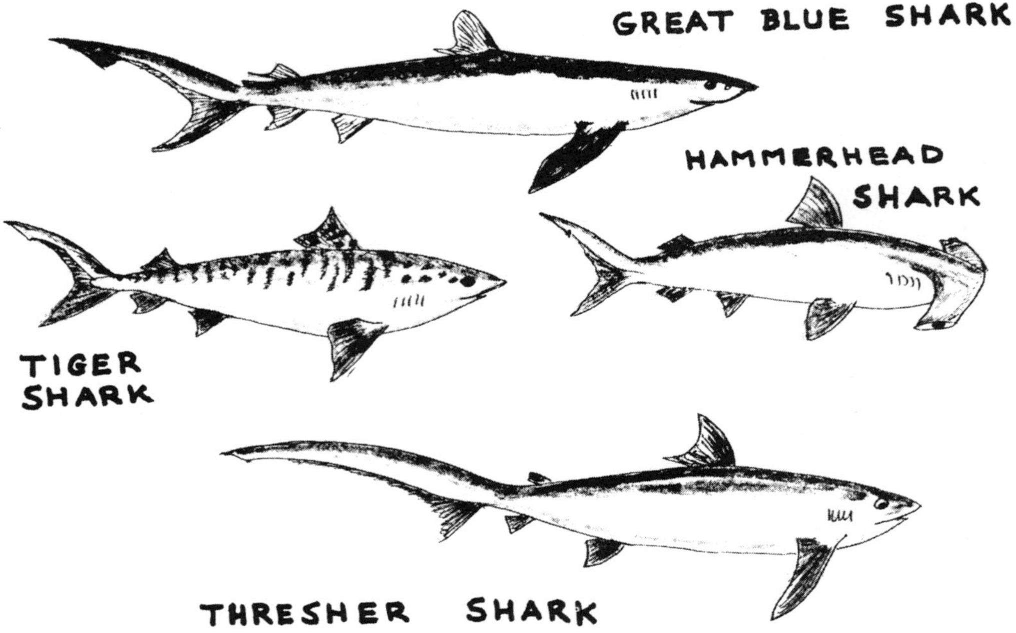
GREAT BLUE SHARK
HAMMERHEAD SHARK
TIGER SHARK
THRESHER SHARK

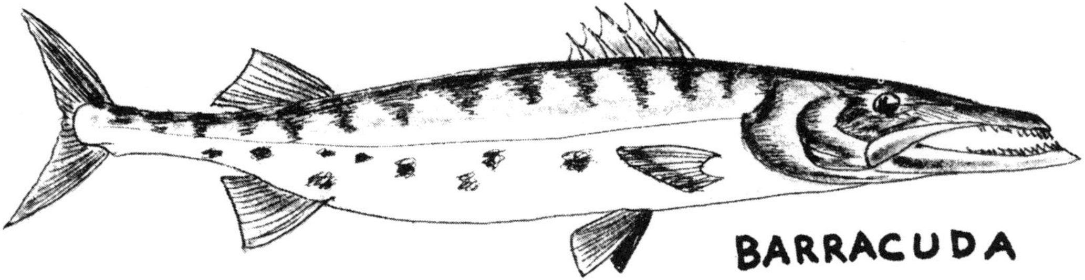

BARRACUDA

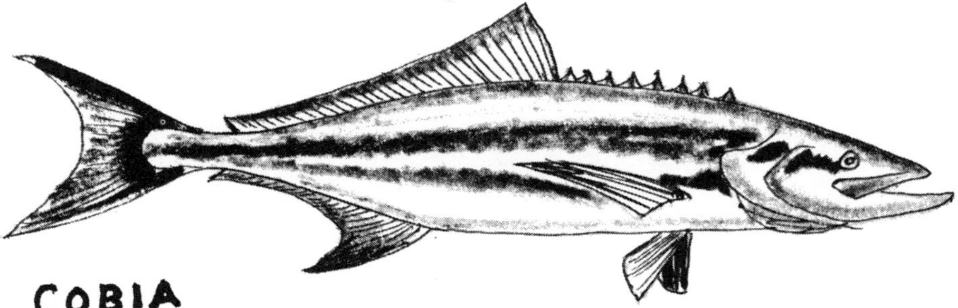

COBIA

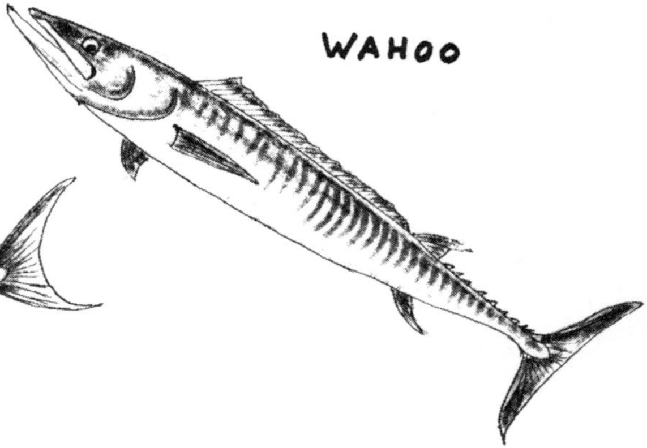

WAHOO

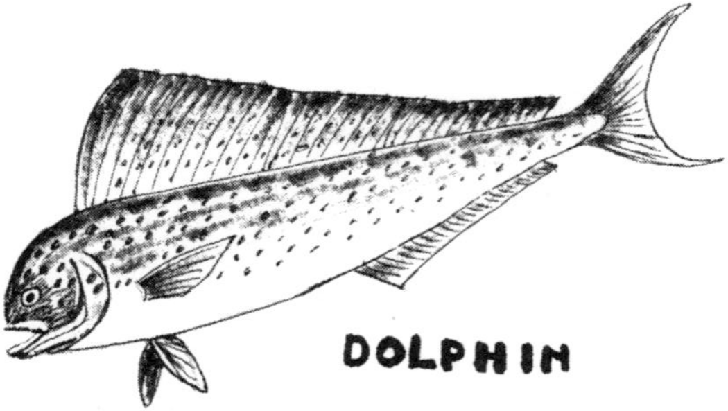

DOLPHIN

FISH OF MOST INTEREST TO SPORTSMEN

Barracuda and Cobia

Fiercest of all saltwater fish with the exception of the shark, the great barracuda (Sphyraena barracuda) of the Atlantic ranges in size from ten to fifty pounds. The Pacific barracuda (Sphyraena argentea) are feared by smaller game and food fish, and have even scared an angler or two by flashing their large, razor-sharp teeth. Both species frequent inshore and beach waters with an occasional visit to the big deep. When taken, it's usually by accident, and most often by big game anglers. Small barracuda are found all season long in southern waters and recently as far north as Cape Cod in the Atlantic. Some prize the meat of the barracuda, but the fierce nature of the fish has held its culinary appeal down. They can be taken in small sizes on conventional light to medium saltwater spinning and boatfishing gear, but the big ones require big game tackle. Their food is anything that moves, including the fisherman.

Wahoo, Dolphin

Not in the least related except for their common grounds, namely, big-deep ocean waters near reefs and drop-offs. The wahoo (Acanthocybium solandei) and the dolphin (Coryphaena hippurus—fish, not the animal variety) range along the southern waters of both coasts all the way to Central America. A big dolphin will weigh from twenty-five to fifty pounds; a wahoo from thirty to sixty pounds. Heavy tackle is needed because they're both rated game fish due to jumping ability and seemingly inexhaustable strength. Baits similar to those used for marlin and other big game fish: bonefish; mackerel; mullet; menhaden. These baits are trolled on the surface and behind the fishing cruiser.

PART II
FRESHWATER BAIT FISHING

5
Techniques for Catching Panfish

MUCH OF THE technique involved in bait fishing is quite similar to that employed when fishing artificial lures and flies, through more care must be exercised to avoid jarring natural bait off the hook. Essentially, bait fishing limits the casting distance, demanding the angler be closer to his target area in order to reach the fish. He has, however, the added enticement of appeal, namely natural foods on which fish feed and a few man-made concoctions to boot!

Panfish are the "little fish," not including any carp that may be encountered in impoundments and reservoirs. And, little fish are the most plentiful and widely distributed. They're readily available so, unless one lives in the Gobi

TECHNIQUES FOR CATCHING PANFISH

Desert, good fishing can probably be found not too far from one's own back porch.

Terminal tackle is as important here as in the case of fishing diverse waters for other species. Lightweight spinning gear, the fly rod and light baitcasting combinations can be used. While the panfisherman will possibly do some casting and trolling, angling for panfish is best done by stillfishing (involving very short casts), and "dunking," that is, walking along the shoreline of a lake or river and tossing the bait out as far as possible. Baits include worms, grasshoppers, frogs, minnows and non-indigenous baits such as porkrind.

BAIT LAKE STILLFISHING

The technique is relatively simple. The lake to be fished may contain sunfish, crappie, bluegill and maybe small bass. There may also be a smattering of white and yellow perch, which is an excellent group to go after. Armed with the terminal rigs, the modern light fly rod or light spinning rod is selected. Locate a portion of the lake either out of the direct wind or where the breeze is blowing away from the shore. Look for indentations in the shoreline where large rocks and boulders, possible grass and lilypad beds, provide ample cover and natural food. Select a location out from the brush and trees to permit free use of the tackle, but not cluttered with water grasses and snags. Cast an unweighted worm, hopper or hooked minnow as far out from shore as possible. Sinkers may not be needed at all. If the current is not too fast nor the water too deep, try to keep the bait as deep as possible without snagging the bottom. The plastic bubble or even a mere bottle cork may be all that is necessary to keep the bait from snagging. If fishing on a lazy-current river, select a quiet deadwater stretch where the bank is high or where rushes form deep holes or pockets.

Catfish and even carp can be rendered on the following baits: For catfish, especially in rivers where the big ones abound, use tasties such as Limburg cheese. Mix it with dough for more holding power on the hook, or use a small plastic bag of see-through thickness and fill it with bait and set it to the hook. Sour meat, clams, rotting fish bait or innards from fish previously caught will work equally as well. If expecting to fish a specific location regularly, try and find dead birds or old meat of any kind; place them in a sack that's weighted down with gravel or stones. Catfish, carp, etc. will flock to it.

DRIFTING, CASTING, TROLLING

The fisherman who owns a small rowboat or canoe, or who can rent one at the lake of his choice should begin by surveying the waters in an excursion cruise. Of course, if the lake or waterway is extensive, such a cruise would depend heavily on individual circumstances and preference. When possible, note where other fishermen are working, and look for stream outlets, deep cut-ins, sheltered coves, sharp points of land, weed-choked bays and rocky shores where the water is reasonably deep. All of these conditions can lead fish to live bait offerings without the need for trolling deep spots or spring holes. When the fishing area has been selected, (and assuming favorable wind direction) rig with minnows or worms, two hooks and a light sinker. Plan to cast this rigging overboard and merely drift along in the breeze. If the course is near shore, drop a line and sinker down once in a while to check the depth. If the lake is fairly shallow, use a bobber adjusted to the correct depth. Upon approaching the shore, a reef or mid-lake grass flat, try anchoring and cast the baits. If the water is deep, say over the ten-foot mark, try trolling slowly, using slightly heavier weights.

ICE FISHING

There's no need to store away fishing gear when the lake freezes over, because then fishing isn't limited to pan or coarse fish. One may catch pike, musky, bass and even trout. Fishing regulations during this period, however, are usually prohibitive and declare "closed season" on most game fish. But fish species illegal by this method in one area may be legal in another. The fisherman should know these laws; neglect them and he'll probably catch cold and a chillier fine!

Tip-ups are generally used for ice fishing. These are simple contraptions baited on lines equipped with a signalling device. This device is designed to alert the angler that a fish is tugging the bait.

It is a cold sport and dreary winter winds will bite reddened noses and chill dispositions. But ice fishing is great fun, especially in the company of fellow anglers with whom to share hot coffee, fishing yarns and tackle techniques. It can be time well spent.

To merely try some fishing luck with a hand line, simply cut a hole in the ice with an axe, drop the baited line into the hole, stand there and wait. The conventional ice-fishing rig is, however, preferred; therefore make several tip-ups and set up a windbreak. Bring along a camp stove, comfortable camp chair and be prepared to sit beneath the winter sky and watch the tip-ups for action.

When the flag goes up this does not necessarily mean the

fish is hooked. It may be merely "fooling around" with the bait. Quite often, if action stops, it's wise to bring the line in and inspect the bait. Part of the ice-fishing technique is to know precisely when to haul back the line to set the hook. Endeavor to wait until the fish starts a full run-off before snubbing him.

INTRODUCE OTHERS TO FISHING PLEASURE

The experience gained by fishing for the somewhat less glamorous panfish is always profitable in fishing for the more active varieties. It helps, for instance, in mastering the choice of tackle and terminal gear, the art of simple short distance casting and the tricks of hooking fish that stubbornly "fool" with the bait. It helps in learning where and how to get the best bait, whether from the field or store-bought. It would be a shame to bungle a potentially thrilling experience with a big bass, trout, pike, musky and even catfish by going unprepared—tacklewise—without regard to the various fishing conditions and gear limitations that are often encountered when the action gets hot.

Over the years, there should be plenty of chance to fish for the "proud ones," but it may come as a surprise to find easy fishing for the smaller species (especially if close to home) a delightful recourse offering many hours of outdoor relaxation.

Where there are youngsters around or neighborhood kids, invite them along—instruct as necessary, and offer them a taste of the good life they might otherwise miss.

For recreation, general education and profitable tips on fishing and outdoor life, it pays to join a rod and gun club.

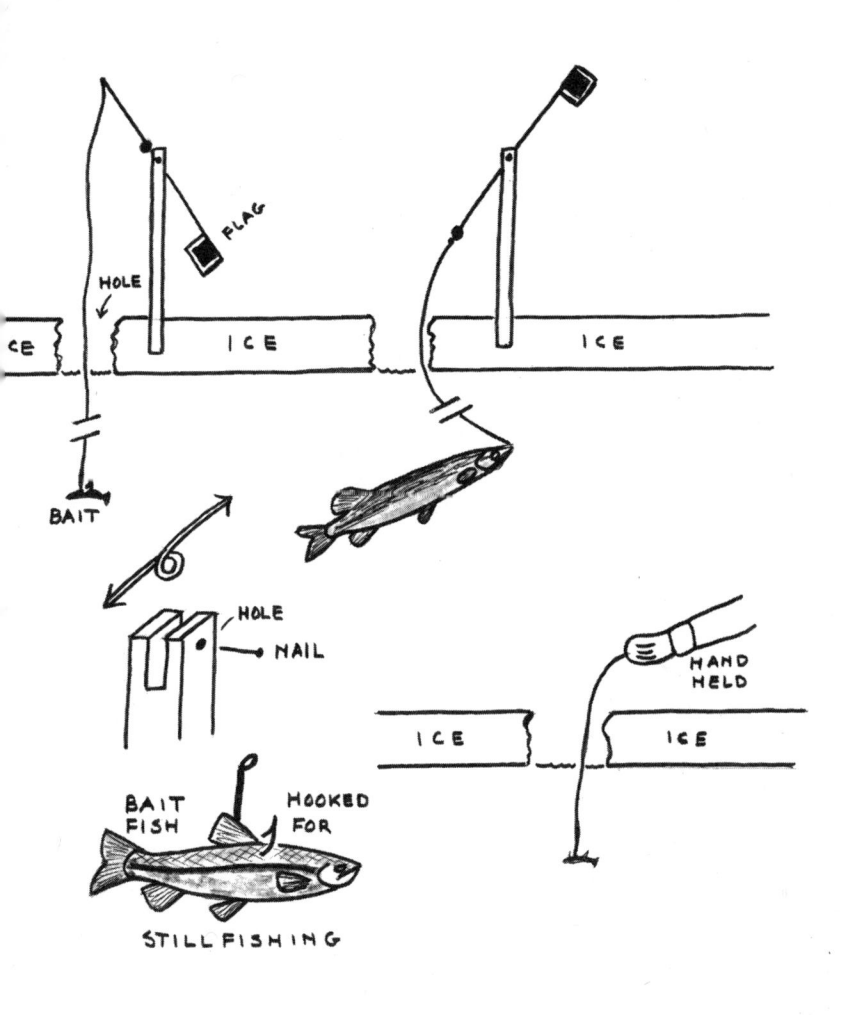

This is the conventional ice fishing rig, showing how it is used.

The exchange of information and feeling of brotherhood in such groups is quite intense. These organizations make sure conservation and anti-pollution efforts are pushed through to the lawmakers. Also, it pays to make a good friend of the game warden, or forest ranger; these fellows can often be very helpful.

6

Bait Fishing Techniques for Freshwater Game Fish

NOW THE BAIT fisherman enters the realm of the "big time"; he's after prize brook, brown, rainbow, steelhead, dolly varden and lake trout; large and smallmouth bass, pickerel, pike, muskellunge and large catfish. That's quite an order, but he's all set, having "rehearsed" much of the technique and tackle selection with smaller fish. He now knows something about where to look for good fishing spots in lakes and rivers. He's familiar with casting, and makes an intelligent choice whether to try drifting, trolling or casting over some specific location with the appropriate tackle. Handling bait has become almost second nature. He's snagged the bottom several times, gotten tangled, lost a few fish by strikes that happened too soon, too hard and too fast. He's lost some from allowing too much slack in the line. In short, he's learned both the agony and ecstasy of bait fishing.

Collecting bait or buying it from local bait and tackle dealers is now a set proposition. When in his boat, he now remembers to place his tackle box out of the way and to stack his rods so they won't get tangled or stepped on. In toto, the routine of fishing is now a part of him and no longer the strange, new project he may once have only dreamt about.

It is time to go after the gamesters and, searching throughout the area in which he lives, he knows what species are available. If he is planning a trip or vacation, he'll head for lakes and rivers that abound with the preferred species.

In this chapter are illustrated various baits, terminal rigs and recommended tackle including suggestions and situations that will help identify the type of waterway and conditions which may be encountered. Many of the rigs shown are probably similar to those the bait fisherman has used before since tackle types constantly overlap when applied to various uses.

In fishing for the game species, however, the accent must be on action. The fisherman will be hooking fish that may grab his bait with ferocious energy and take off before he will have had time to react or prepare. Or, the fish may lazily mouth the bait, necessitating the patience to hold back before setting the hook. Playing these fish requires working knowledge gained from experience in tackle use. One learns just how far to strain the rod, especially with those lively ones that can either run all the line out in fast water or take terminal gear to the bottom and snag it in order to escape the menacing hook.

The terrific power of a one-pound rainbow trout or a four-pound largemouth bass is amazing. And a ten-pound pike will give turbulent battle. With luck (one of the few times it's needed) you may even land a twenty-five pound musky!

There will also be days when no matter how well the fisherman handles his tackle he'll probably return home fishless. Somehow even fish have their "day of rest," and simply refuse to nibble. Fishing, like other sports, has its delightful frustrations.

LARGE OR SMALLMOUTH BASS

Large and smallmouth bass are primarily lake fish though the smallmouth is often found in fast streams. Depending on the conditions, fishing methods are: casting, trolling, still and drift fishing. When the lakes are high in the spring, cast to or troll by the shorelines directly into the grass and overhangs. As the season progresses and where legal, bass can be taken in their spawning grounds by casting and/or trolling. Later, they will be found during the early morning hours and at night along the shore, or deep in the cold-temperature belts and spring holes by still or drift fishing. Earthworms, nightcrawlers and live bait such as yellow perch (a fish with more stamina than the minnow) or frogs are strongly recommended. Crawfish are excellent, cast unweighted at dusk or nightime along the grassy shore where there are holes among the rocks.

Seek protected bays and coves for casting and sharp points of land for trolling and stillfishing. When fishing an unfamiliar lake, inquire about the hot spots at the local tackle store and chew the fat with fellow anglers at the boat dock. Observe where other anglers fish and how they are doing it, particularly those who come into the dock with loaded fish stringers!

When night fishing from the shore, make sure to walk the

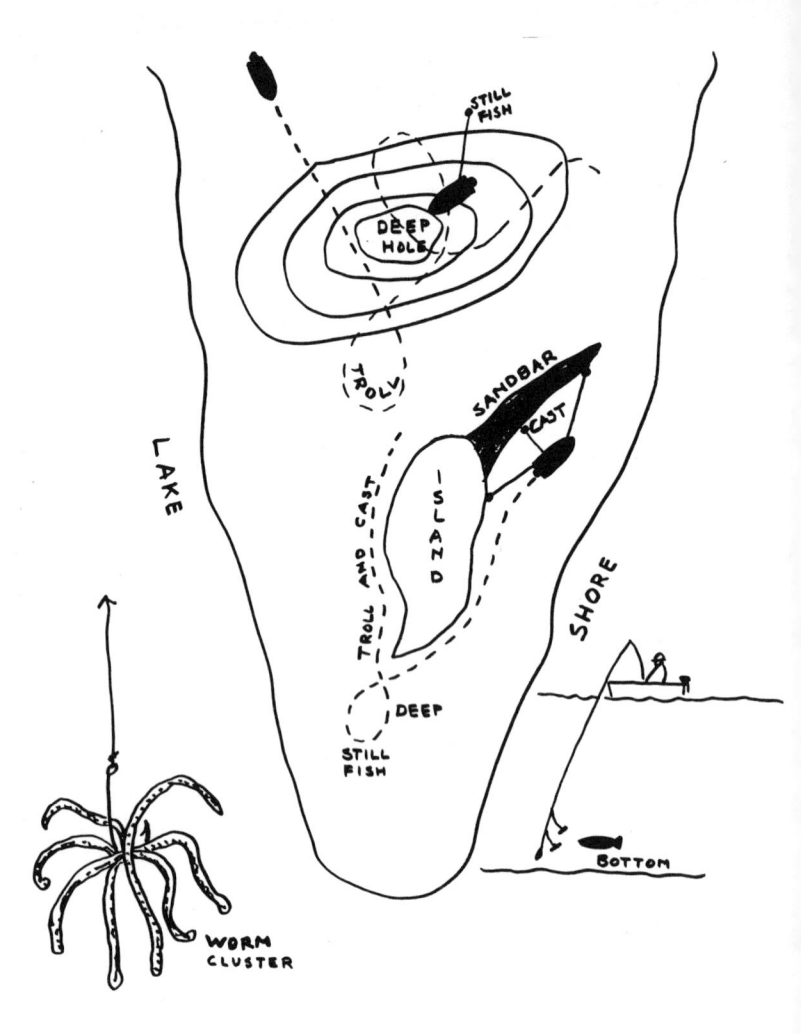

More techniques for casting, retrieving and trolling—how and where to baitfish under various circumstances (see also next page).

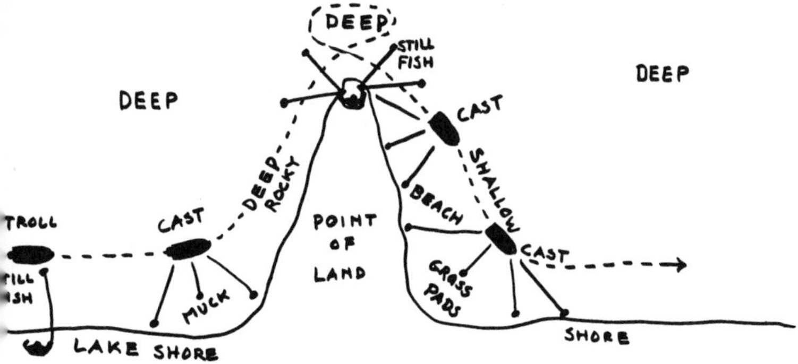
DEEP
STILL FISH
DEEP
DEEP
CAST
DEEP ROCKY
SHALLOW
BEACH
TROLL
CAST
POINT OF LAND
CAST
GRASS PADS
MUCK
LAKE SHORE
SHORE

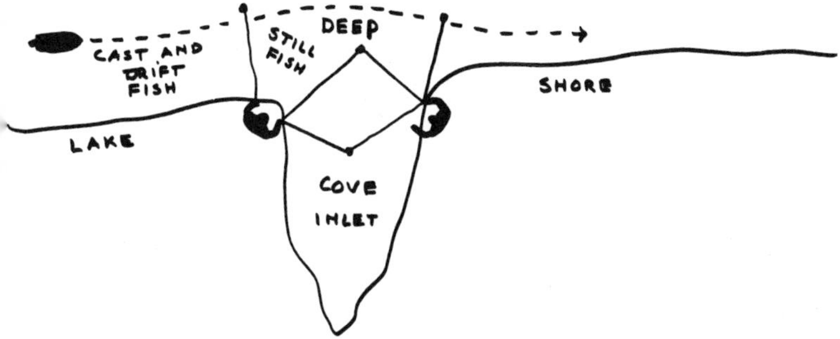
DEEP
STILL FISH
CAST AND DRIFT FISH
SHORE
LAKE
COVE INLET

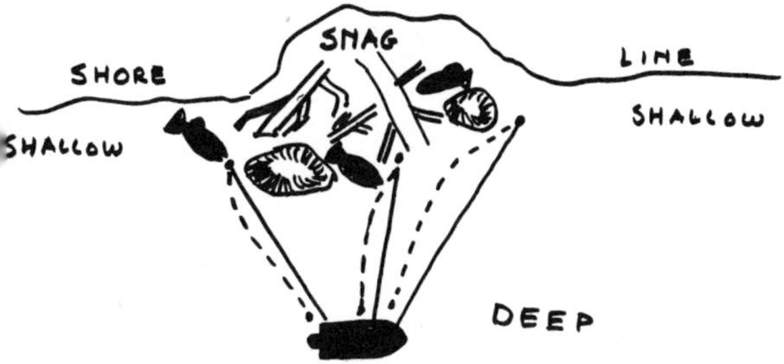
SNAG
SHORE
LINE
SHALLOW
SHALLOW
DEEP

shoreline the day before. *Do not venture into a strange territory after dark.* When fishing from a boat at night keep light to a minimum, because even a dim flash scares bass and blinds the fisherman for minutes afterward. Learn to tie knots and select pre-arranged terminal tackle and bait without having to use a light; fishermen who can do this will be much better off. Remember not to go out alone; always take a friend when fishing at night. This is generally the best time to fish the big ones during the hot summer since they seem to bite oftener at night.

TROUT

Trout fishing in lakes is a tricky proposition. During the early season just after the ice is out, trout surface for a few weeks, feeding on small flies and minnows. Take them with unweighted baits such as worms, nymphs, impaled insects and live minnows, by casting, near-surface trolling or drift fishing. Mornings or evenings when the wind is down are the best times and groups of trout can be found where they feed.

Trout of the big rivers will be found in the slackwaters, below bends and in big, deep pools. Since there is some current action, dead minnows can be used though live ones are frequently better.

As the season progresses, lake trout will seek the cool waters of stream outlets or spring holes. Locate these areas and troll across them, dropping the baits to various depths. During the summer, river trout will similarly seek out aerated water, so fish for them directly below the breaks in rapids and in fast-water slicks.

Light to medium gear is required, though heavy weights may not be needed as terminal tackle unless one plans to work the deepest portions of the lake. Here again, find out as much as can be learned from the "locals" and consult geodetic maps for lake contours. Use a thermometer, seek depths where temperatures range from sixty to seventy degrees. Knowing the proper depth is most important in lake fishing, especially during the summer season. Night, or at least pre-dawn fishing is preferred if there is heavy boating activity during the day.

All manner of aquatic insects can be used; don't neglect the grasshopper.

LAKE TROUT AND WALLEYE PIKE

Quite often these two species are found in the same lake. They're both bait fishing exclusives though they can be enticed with artificial lures, too. Best combination for casting and medium trolling is a spoon or set of spinners followed by cut fish bait or rigged dead minnow. Only in the spring will these two be taken near the surface and usually near stream outlets. Fish for them in deep water by very slow trolling, using wire lines and heavy sinkers for bait; or sinkers, spoons, spinners and bait. The medium-weight baitcasting rod, or specialized trolling rod is an excellent choice, either with level-wind baitcasting reel or large-capacity spinning reel.

Since these fish are found in big lakes, there is a great deal of territory to explore. One may spend an entire season in blind fishing and never hit the hot spots. But as suggested in previous pages, cull information from every available source. The conservation offices of the various states have excellent publications and distribute current fishing reports for the particular state, including stocking dates and general condi-

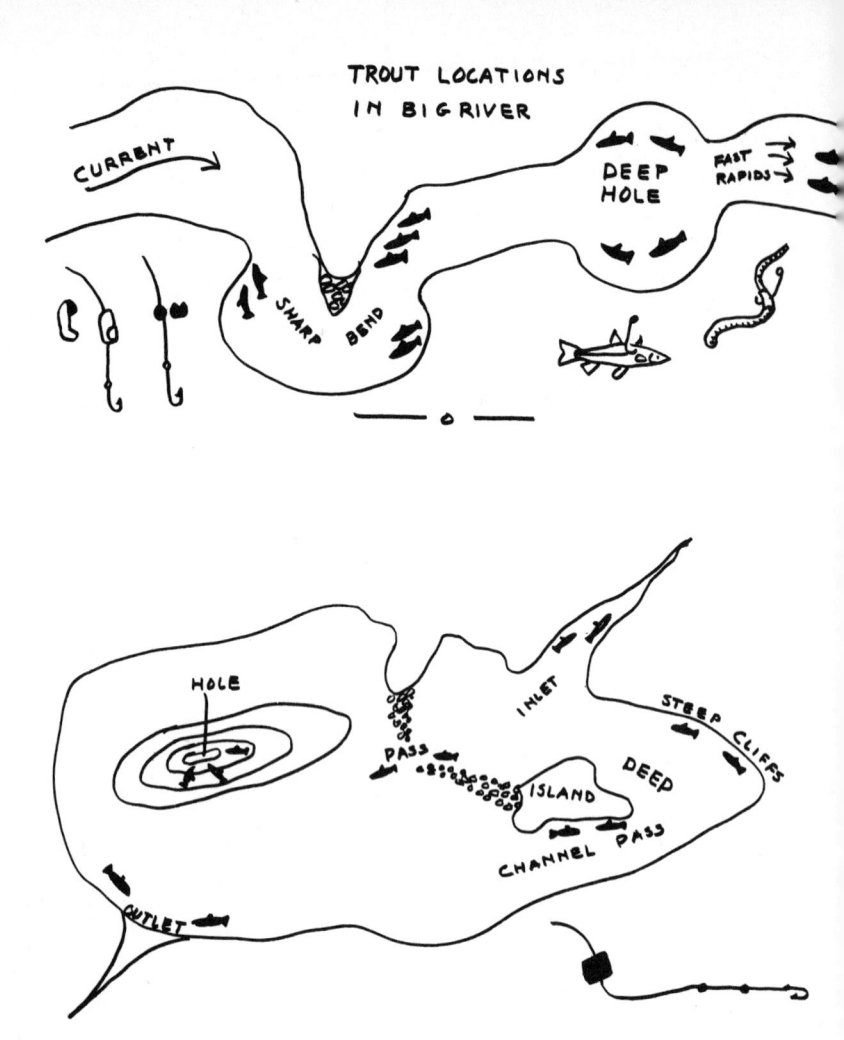

Techniques for trout in lakes and rivers vary quite a bit according to the size of water and season of the year. Here are some standard approaches.

BAIT FISHING TECHNIQUES—FRESHWATER GAME FISH 99

tions. Write to them. Resort owners must keep informed and up-to-date with regard to such information for the benefit of their patrons. So don't be afraid to ask about the hot spots; bone up also on rigs and tackle combinations that are paying off, locally.

Lake fishing can be a boring and unrewarding proposition when fishing over barren waters. So the most important part of this fishing will be to inquire first and fish later. A good source of information are places selling bait. Also when possible watch the anglers in nearby boats and (without being too obvious) try to fish near where they're hauling 'em in.

PIKE AND MUSKY

Now, combine what's been related about trout, bass, lake trout and walleye. Then to be all set, go equipped with much heavier gear. These two fish, the biggest and fiercest, are found in lakes, fast and slow rivers and interlinked streams. Their homeland, generally in northern country, abounds with brush-cluttered streams and shorelines littered with driftwood, snags and big bouldered coves and bays. The best seasons are spring and fall.

These are big fish and require a hardy morsel to attract them. While artificial lures take big ones once in a while, the bait fisherman really has the edge if he goes with adequate tackle to handle the presentation of the bait and the power of the fish. Small catfish and lake chubs are the best baits. The deeper they are fished, the better! Troll, stillfish or cast, depending on conditions.

The strike of a big fish is liable to be harsh and sudden, especially to trolled bait. If stillfishing, these fish will mouth

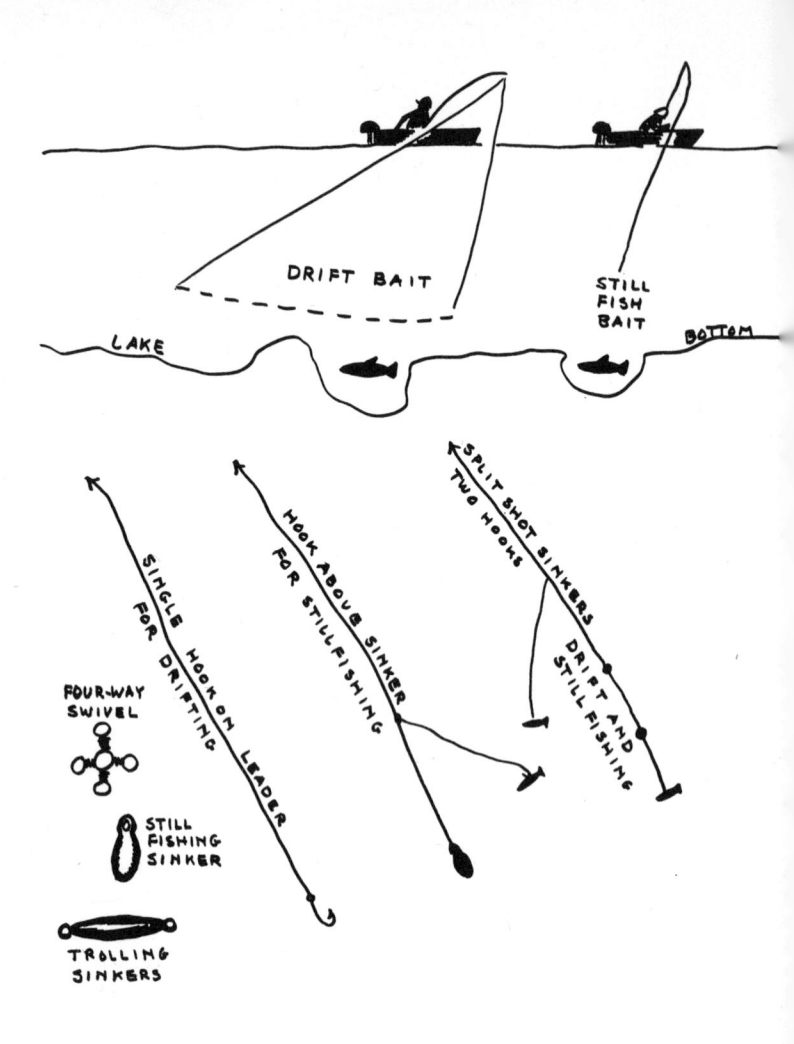

Lake trout and walleyes are taken deep down most of the year. This is the way to do it and the rigs to use.

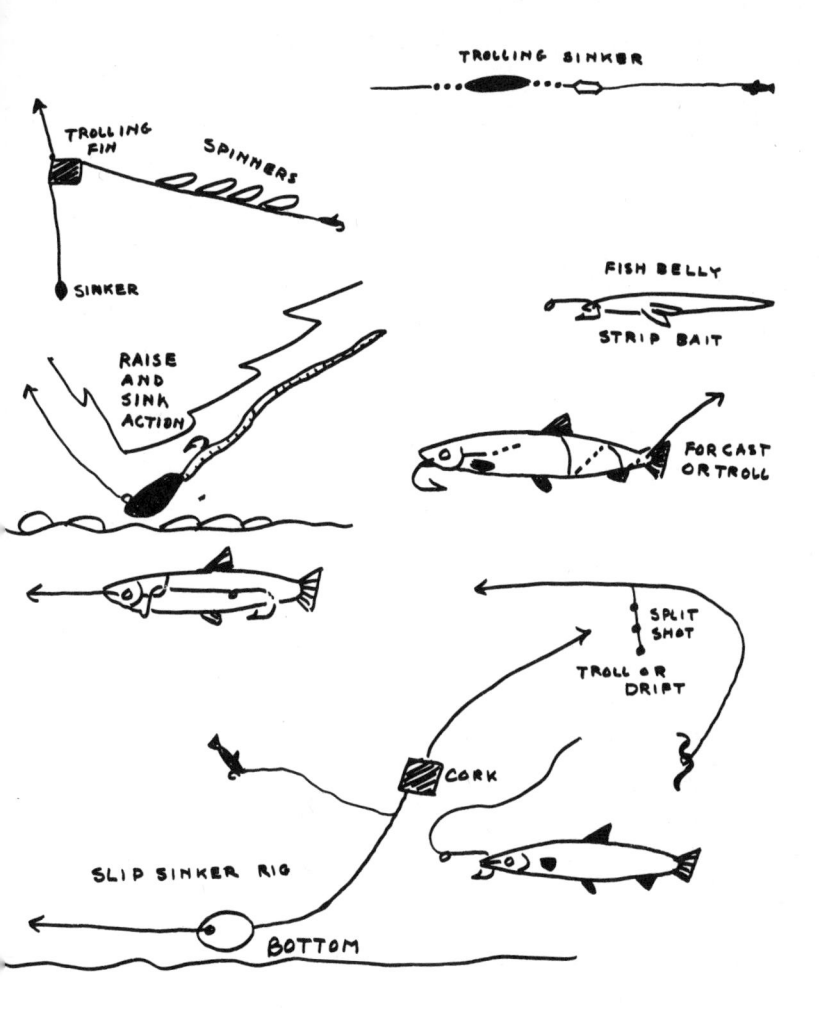

The pike and musky fisherman must be able to fish very deep as well as up near the surface. Here are shown appropriate rigs for the bait-fisherman that will enable him to do either.

the bait before taking it, but once they do, the action starts with a bang. Stay with it and hold on for dear life.

When landing either species remember they are big and strong, with a mouthful of razor-sharp teeth able to tear up the landing net in a single swipe and inflict mighty gashes on the fisherman's legs or hands. Club them over the head and shoot them if necessary. But make certain they're dead before reaching near the fish's mouth to extricate the hook. Use a long-handled hook-extractor or a pair of pliers.

Terminal-tackle requirements are simple. Use adequate weights in the form of spoons and/or spinners ahead of the bait for casting or trolling with plastic-covered wire leaders to the hook.

STEELHEAD

This species of trout requires a different technique, terminal tackle and bait than is customary under ordinary circumstances. Steelhead occupy the rivers of the Pacific Coast behind the salmon in a lusty quest for salmon eggs that have failed upstream spawning. Theirs is a constant diet of these eggs and as a result, they give little attention to other foods. Even when they can feed on other natural stream foods, these trout still prefer salmon eggs.

The salmon eggs drift down from above individually or in clusters, so it is up to the angler to duplicate this occurrence as best he can. Where salmon eggs are legal for use as bait, they are merely impaled on a very small hook as singles or doubles.

Clusters of salmon eggs or, if not available, steelhead eggs can be used as shown.

Only during the season when salmon are absent will the

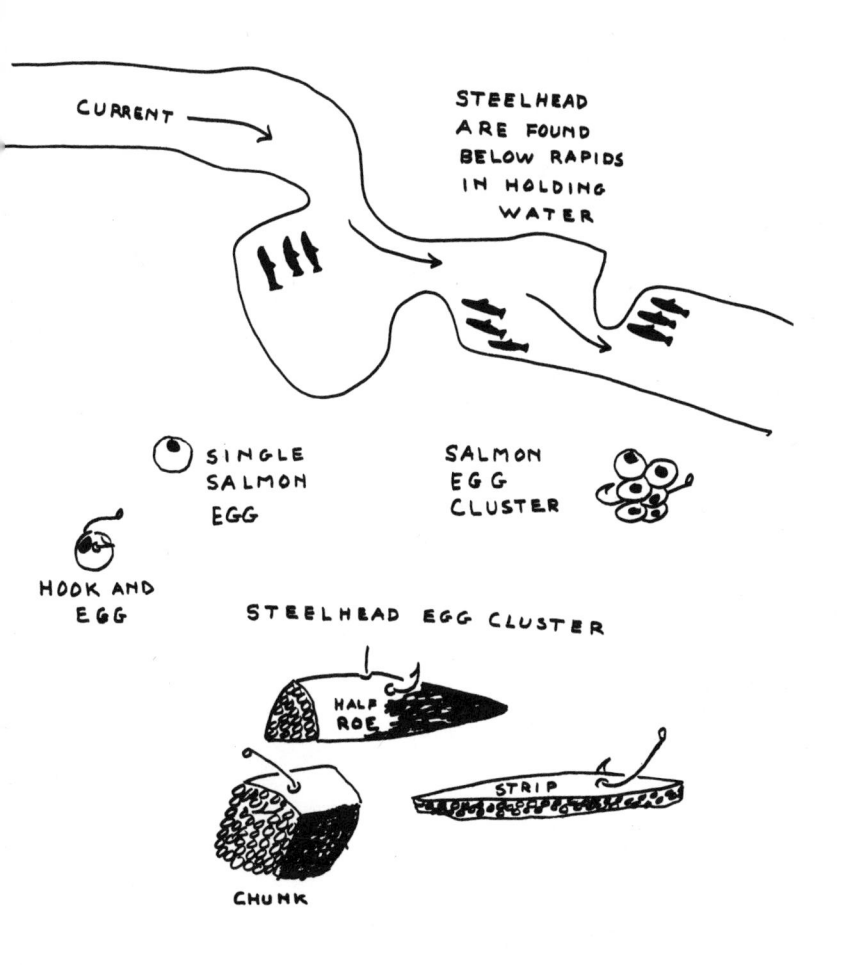

Illustrating appropriate bait rigs for steelhead fishing and suggested places for stream fishing.

resident steelhead take any interest at all in minnows or other baits. The standard standby is always mother earthworm, and it's best when all else fails.

Once hooked to a steelhead, the fisherman is in for some high jumps not unlike the kingly Atlantic salmon. He should be prepared for long runs and surface body rolls—keep his rod tip raised and the line as clear of obstructions as possible. For steelhead, always go equipped with sturdy tackle and plenty of reserve line. Fish for them from Northern California to British Columbia. These trout are plentiful in most coastal streams and the main trick is to be right there on the stream when a good "run" is on.

7

Bait Stream Fishing in Brook and Creek

BAIT FISHING IN streams and brooks differs radically from fishing in the still water of ponds and lakes. The most important factor is the current. Baits have to be cast and manipulated to drift naturally in the current lanes, and via these routes into holes and pockets. Baits are mostly aquatic, that is, stream-bred insects and shellfish in their nymphal or larval stage of development.

BAITS THAT CATCH FRESHWATER FISH

The mayfly, stonefly and caddis nymphs and larvae represent food common to most stream fish. These are shown in the accompanying illustrations. These also show their adult or flying stage. They're gotten underwater by disturbing the rocks and gravel in the stream with one's feet while holding a fine net or wire screen down-current of the disturbance to catch the insects. They don't live long in still water such as in a belt bait-holder, but this is not as important as with minnows, which should be alive if they are to be most effective. The supply of these insects is greatest in the early spring before hatching and they can be had during the entire legal fishing season. These insects are an inch long or under, making it necessary to impale them carefully on small hooks and to cast them gently.

Fish in streams, creeks and brooks feed also on the various species of dace, stream shiners, minnows and frogs which form the rest of their natural diet, hence they are valuable as live bait. They are gathered by the use of minnow traps or fine mesh nets which can be used to catch a few at a time. These can be lured into a side pocket along the stream by using bread crumbs or bits of meat. Bait dealers sell the local species of minnow and it's best to buy a few at a time, keeping them in a minnow bucket, submerged in the stream, and carrying along only a few in a belt bucket for actual fishing. Other live baits to be relied upon are the angleworm, nightcrawler or frog and, failing this, land-bred insects such as grasshoppers, crickets and moths can also be caught and used. Unnatural baits which are effective: cheese, corn and porkrind.

Earthworms

The earthworm is the oldest and most potent freshwater bait. It is easier to get and more often used than any other bait.

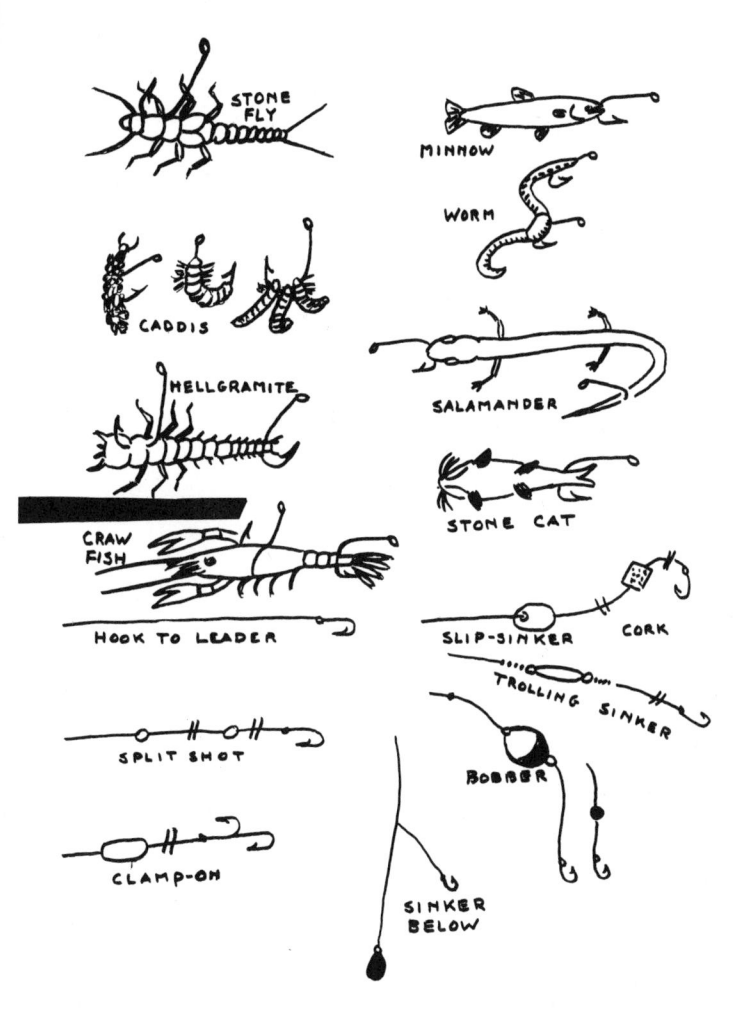

Suggested natural baits for brook, stream and creek fishing and how to rig them with the right terminal tackle. Don't overlook using frogs, either!

The best earthworms are those taken from manure piles or from very damp and fertile soil. They can be used as is, but it's advisable to pack them in damp moss overnight. This eliminates dirt that worms absorb, hardening them somewhat and giving them a reddish color. Keep them in a cool place such as a can or bottle and make sure they have enough air by poking holes into the container.

There is a "collar" on the earthworm which is tougher than the rest of its body. This is the section through which the hook should be inserted.

Earthworms are washed into streams by sudden freshets of water or rain. As bait, they are particularly effective immediately following a rainstorm.

Nightcrawlers

Nightcrawlers are nothing more than big earthworms. At night these are easily gotten during the summer months by seeking them on well-kept lawns such as those found at golf courses. Use a flashlight and grab them before they head for refuge, which they can do with considerable zest. Keep them cool in moss, grass and dirt—an airy container with good circulation is a must.

Like the earthworm, these, too, have a tough collar which is the base for inserting the hook or hooks. They are much easier to keep on the hook than earthworms so larger hooks can be used.

There is an old belief that a big fish enjoys a mouthful, and the nightcrawler is a might big mouthful for most stream fish. However, mastering the dead drift technique described later on is necessary for fishing them effectively. The nightcrawler is also available from local bait dealers and usually on hand at many tackle stores. As with earthworms, it

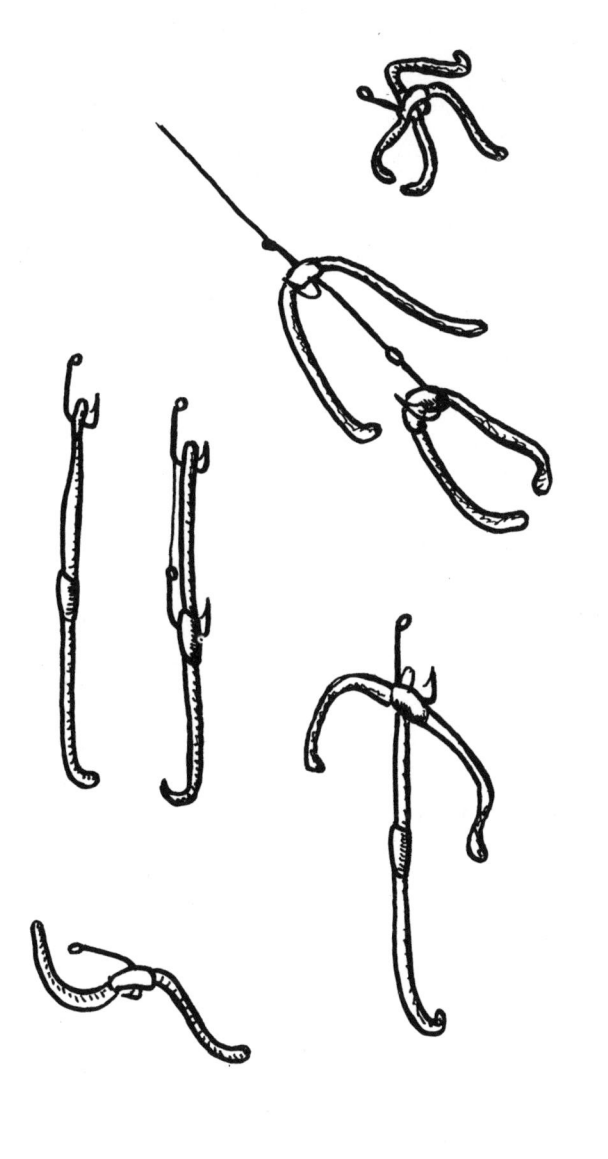

Ways to rig earthworms for all kinds of fishing conditions.

is best to fish with these when they are alive and "wiggly." A dead worm has little appeal to either angler or fish.

Live Minnows

As stated earlier, live minnows are the best, even though more care is needed to keep them alive. If the belt baitbucket is kept constantly replenished with fresh water and the base pail cool and refreshed, minnows will live longer and be livelier on the hook. Caution must be taken in handling them for the hooking process. Try not to squeeze them, even if they slither about in the hand while being hooked.

Elsewhere in this book is a dictionary of baits and the various species will be found in northern streams, particularly the trout streams and the slightly larger redbelly minnow in southern streams. Stream shiners and a host of small minnows are constantly available for catching or buying. The main point here is to concentrate on the type of hooking to be done—do it carefully and then proceed to cast the bait without flipping it off or killing it by slapping it down too hard on the water's surface. Dragging it too fast on the retrieve can also drown the minnow, so retrieve it slowly.

Dead Minnow Cut Bait

While the dead minnow does not have the appeal of the live one, it is nonetheless still a good bait for stream fishing. This is particularly true in slower streams that contain all species of bass and panfish, plus bigger game fish such as walleyes, pickerel, pike and muskellunge. In fact, large suckers or shiners are rigged dead for trolling and casting for pike and muskellunge. Walleyes too, will go for dead baits. Catfish, carp and other coarse fish will also devour dead

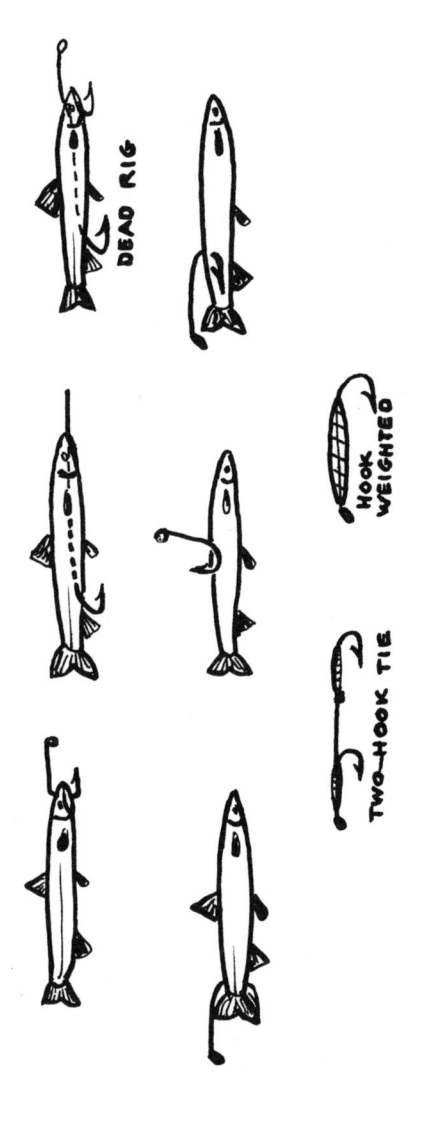

There are numerous ways of baiting-up with live minnows. Care must be taken to hook the minnow so that it stays alive as long as possible; furthermore, it should be rigged so that it does not spin when cast or trolled. Here are some standard riggings.

minnows and minnows cut into bits or sections. Impale the bait carefully and firmly because these fish are great bait-stealers, especially the catfish.

There are numberless ways of hooking and rigging dead minnows. Shown here are the most popular. It is wise, when fishing unfamiliar waters, to consult the local bait store or tackle shop. If using a guide, take his advice and glean as much valuable information as can be had. Somebody is always coming up with a better method.

Aquatic Insects

The stonefly, in its aquatic form, is one of the best of three major insect species for bait fishing trout and smallmouth bass. True, dobson and damsel fly larvae are also available, but not in as great supply. These last are more common on the slower streams where mud and muck roll along the shoreline. In typical gravel, boulder-strewn trout streams, the stonefly is the easiest to catch. During the months of May, June and July, you will see the empty cocoon-like cases of these insects along the shoreline of the stream. These are the shells of insects hatched the night before.

The live insect is a potent one for trout. They can be gathered by overturning rocks and gravel at the heads of pools and along the deeper drop-offs under water. They scamper very quickly so even the net will miss unless one is quick. The adult fly, as stated, hatches at night, while most of the useful mayflies hatch during the daytime. So, those who wish to try night fishing can, with the aid of a flashlight, find the adult flies as they hatch along the stream edge or mid-stream rocks. Gather them quickly after hatching and keep them in a secure container. Use dead or alive since in this

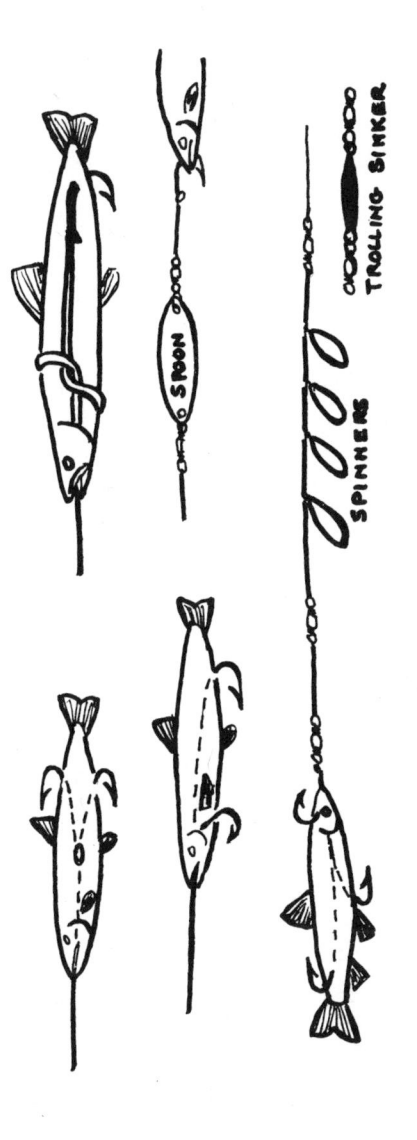

Dead minnow bait rigs are legion. Shown here are two standard ways. Cut minnows or slips of flesh from either a minnow or a caught fish are also rigged like these.

case it doesn't really matter, and hook through the "collar" as shown.

Mayfly nymphs, particularly the larger sizes, are preferred and should be used with very small hooks. In the adult (flying) stage, they are much too soft for hooking and casting. Other insects discussed in previous pages including crawfish are preferred bait where they are native to the stream.

Land-bred Insects as Bait

Here you have numerous choices of insects which, if they can be caught, are excellent tempters of game fish, especially trout and bass. For fishing in the early morning or evening there's nothing better than a succulent, large moth caught beneath your porch light, the night before. And moths are also good daytime baits.

The grasshopper is an excellent bait as it has a fairly stiff collar for easy and more secure hooking. It resembles the stonefly, and fish consequently gobble them up with gusto. Best time to catch hoppers is when the dew is still on the ground in the early morning hours. They're not so lively then and they can be caught by the can-full in a few minutes in any nearby field. When fishing, throw a few into the water and watch them drift downstream on the currents. If a fish swirls the fisherman knows he's in business. Another one should be immediately offered, this one with a hook in it. The same can be done with crickets.

When they are in season, caterpillars represent a major recourse to the fish's diet. They're easily gathered, especially where their white nests can be spotted in nearby trees along the stream. The green caterpillar is a favorite in June in the northern states.

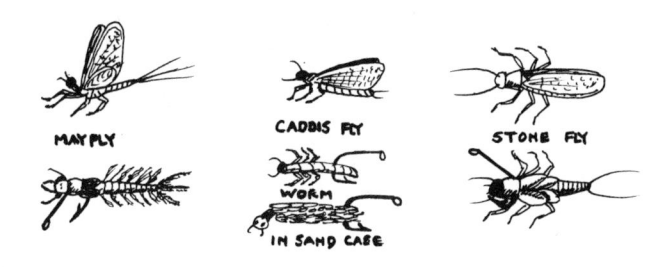

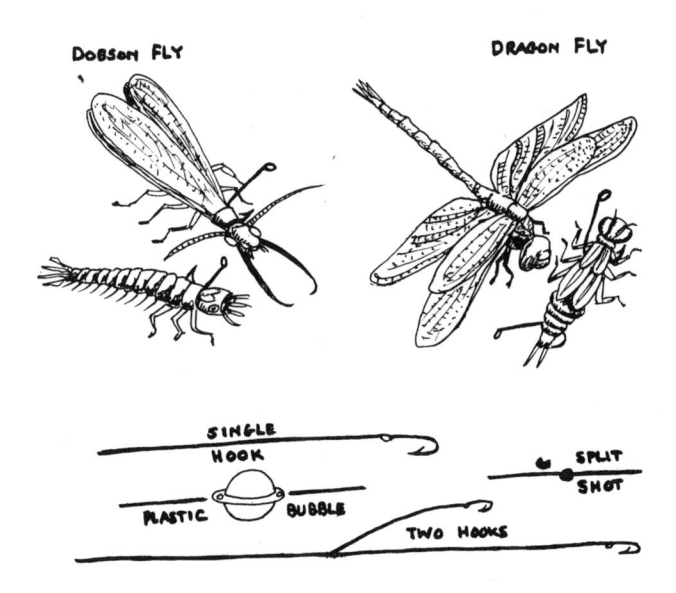

Aquatic insects are numerous in species, varied in their appeal to the fish and relative value to the fisherman. Shown here are some of the standard ways of rigging them to the hook with appropriate terminal tackle.

Unnatural Baits

For many years, porkrind has lead the list of so-called "unnatural" baits in both lake and stream fishing for all species of game fish. Pork fat seems to have its strong appeal and remains potent long after submersion. The tough rind also provides secure hooking strength. Pork chunk, as it is called, is cut in various ways for casting and drifting in the current. Easy to come by, and easy to keep in a cool container.

Cheese, bits of American and mild cheddar, simply thrill bass and trout, particularly in the Western states where they have gained intense popularity as game-fish bait. And cheese has always been a favorite with catfish and carp. Just sink a hook into it and drop the works overboard.

Single kernels of corn are excellent bait for trout and mostly in the early spring, while spawning goes on upstream. Evidently, trout mistake corn for trout eggs, or so goes the theory. But single kernels of corn on tiny hooks are most effective, more so than the traditional earthworm would be under similar circumstances. Later in the season, corn can be relied upon to take trout and panfish with regularity.

TERMINAL RIGS

While the terminal rigs for stream fishing are somewhat similar to those used in casting and stillfishing on lakes and slow rivers, the technique is different due to the existence of current.

Remember you are working with very light, soft baits. This requires a rod with limber tip-action, whether it be fly or spinning rod. Most baitcasting rods are too stiff for this kind of fishing with the exception of casting heavier-rigged dead baits and rigged minnows.

BAIT STREAM FISHING

There are several ways of rigging the terminal weights and bobbers with one or two hooks. Remember selected baits can always be used in conjunction with single or double Indiana or Colorado spinners. Bait is also used with spoons and various spinning lures by way of added attraction.

With the advent of spinning, the plastic bubble was devised for fishing with lightweight bait. It can also be used effectively with the fly rod.

FISHING TECHNIQUE

The technique to use while fishing streams is primarily the "dead drift" method. If the bait merely hangs in the current unnaturally, it tends to spin to the surface. This is all right if the fish are very hungry, but for the bigger fish and those in heavily fished water, the closer the effect to natural drift of loose bait carried by the current, the better will be the results.

This means, when casting from shore or wading, that the cast should be made as shown in the accompanying illustrations in a quartering upstream direction, the path of the bait pre-planned to drift down through a run—that is, by a rock, snag, into a deep hole or under an overhanging bank. In shallow streams where the current is fast, the bait will not sink rapidly unless slightly weighted; however, too much weight and there will be snagging. In deeper, slower water, weights should be kept to a minimum because slower current will allow the bait to drop down. Only in extremely fast water should heavy weights be used. The fisherman must learn by trial and error. He must develop his judgment and be willing to change weights to suit the problems at hand.

Basically, bait should drop as low to the bottom as possible without interruptions of drift caused by catching on the bottom. Shown here are some of the preferred sinkers and rigs. Note in some cases that a lighter strand of leader is used when the weight is at the end of the line. This way, if the weight snags the bottom, the leader may break, losing the sinkers, but saving the rig.

The retrieve can and should be across the stream, across the main currents, and behind rocks and snags. The final reel-in should be slow since quite often fish will follow a bait around the circular retrieve and pounce on it only as it reaches the limit of its drift or as its retrieve is begun—often just as it is at the point of being whisked away.

Direct downstream baiting should be done by merely dropping the bait below the rod tip and allowing it to be tugged by the current. Where one can wade into the stream well above a rock or hot spot, and allow the bait to drift naturally down to the rock, this will appear as natural food drift to the fish. A good time for the fisherman to be prepared for a hefty strike!

DRIFT FISHING

This type of baiting can be done best by walking along the shore, the current stretch alongside, or from a boat controlled in its drift by oars, paddle or pole. Weights should be chosen that will get the bait down to the fish in a natural drift and not in a "pulled" position wherein the bait constantly tries to rise to the surface. Fishing from a boat, speed is the determining factor in depth and drift control.

As to the rig, some prefer the bait to drift *after* the weight, while others prefer it *before* the weight. Either way is satisfactory.

BAIT STREAM FISHING

The fisherman casts to the side as far as he can and, if waterbound, has the boat held solidly for a moment while the bait tumbles through the current in a circular swing across the stream to the front and side of him respectively. The retrieve should be *very* slow in order to lure fish that may be following.

In very fast water, cast the rig on an upstream angle to cover more water and allow the bait to sink deeper.

Drift fishing where the current carries the bait faster than the boat, is truly the easiest to accomplish. Synchronize boat speed with current speed and the bait will drift beautifully into the holes and runs.

The rod is held flat to the water, but the drag is set to extremely light pressure. For the strike, the line should be cushioned. If the rod is held high, the bait tends to rise and remain on the surface.

STILLFISHING

In this all one needs to do is locate a deep hole along the stream, a quiet water pocket in a bend or a long, quiet, slow stretch of water. Cast the bait and terminal rig into the water and let nature take its course. Allow the bait to sink down, but not snag the bottom.

Stillfishing requires a soft-tipped rod for easy, short-distance casting. Terminal rigs are similar to those used in lake stillfishing: one or two hooks on leaders (separated to avoid tangling) and a sinker. A slipping cork or bobber is set at a fixed position on the line, its proper place being measured to permit the bait a depth close to the bottom (directly *on* the bottom would risk a snag). Live worms, minnows or frogs are preferable baits since these swim around with satisfactory liveliness.

Another rig is the slip-sinker, with or without a bobber. As the fish pulls on the bait, the line slips through a hole in the sinker. This allows the fish a good long run before it is snubbed and it allows time to make sure that it has taken the bait securely.

Set the reel drag to light; prop the rod up on a forked stick and muse until something happens.

When a long rod is required in stillfishing, use a 9½ ft. fly rod equipped with either a closed-face spinning reel or a single-action fly reel. The old-style cane pole system is outmoded and unnecessary for the one or two-rod angler.

Fishing conditions and fish species are more varied in streams than in lakes. But no two portions of a stream are the same, nor do they offer the same interesting situations. Game fish vary from the three favorite trout; brown, brook and rainbow; the bass, large and smallmouth; pickerel, perch, crappie, rock bass, walleye pike, northern pike, musky, catfish and carp. As seasons change, natural, aquatic, land-bred and unnatural baits can be used interchangeably. Their use is governed only by the angler's desire to catch and keep natural baits, coupled with the availability of such baits at the location.

One can fish streams by walking the shore or wading in the shallows. When wading broad streams or rivers, trustworthy chest-high waders are recommended. Fish all day; fish all night, the pleasures are constant and as fresh as the sport itself.

It is best for the angler to go equipped with terminal rigs prepared in advance, neatly coiled and labeled in the tackle box. This will save time on the water. Baits should be kept in

BAIT STREAM FISHING

containers that permit good ventilation and cool conditions. Hooks should be sharp and knots kept tied securely.

Bait fishing—especially in streams—is more interesting than artificial-lure fishing inasmuch as this way the fisherman is offering the fish foods it likes, even though he may have to work a little in obtaining them. His tackle is geared for the task at hand, and this fishing demands a good caster who knows the proper techniques and manipulations so that the fish will look upon his bait offerings as entirely natural, convenient, attractive, and without suspicion.

8
Catching, Keeping and Carrying Live Bait

CATCHING, KEEPING AND carrying bait can be almost as much fun as the actual fishing. It is instructive to youngsters and any fisherman. There's much of interest concerning natural baits, their stages of growth and environment.

For the catching of minnows, crawfish and frogs, the bait hunter must familiarize himself with the shoreline where bait and game fish feed, spawn and live. From this he will "learn" the stream and its nymphs and larvae, all valuable information which he may use in the same pools or runs in later fishing action.

Gathering worms and land insects can be fun and similarly instructive. Find them in damp acid ground, manure piles, and in compost.

CATCHING, KEEPING AND CARRYING LIVE BAIT 123

When gathering these invaluable creatures, don't wantonly waste them; take only what is needed and keep them alive—these will produce great fishing action. Certain equipment is needed to catch, transport and preserve bait for stream or boat fishing. Today, the tackle industry has produced top-quality equipment for this important side-aspect of the fishing sport. See your dealer.

A worm box made with screen wire can be your worm "factory," or you can set aside a section of the garden. After introducing worms, keep the earth moist and work in compost and cornmeal to help feed them. Mail-order companies advertising in the various sport magazines sell both bait and equipment for raising worms and other baits.

To condition worms, place them in damp sand for a few hours. They will scour themselves and become tough and redder.

Live frogs are excellent bass baits and will catch other fish as well. "Frog harnesses," convenient for baiting up with frogs, are available at many tackle stores. Frogs may be fished either shallow or deep, or "skittered" across the tops of lily pads.

AQUATIC INSECTS

These are the most difficult to keep alive, but one can attempt to keep them overnight for the following day's fishing. They consist of stonefly larvae, caddis fly larvae, mayfly nymphs, dobson flies, hellgramites and whatever "wormy looking" aquatic insects one chances to collect. But check local fishing laws. Collection of these insects is frequently prohibited in certain locations.

The dragon or dobson fly larvae is one of the best and

strongest. Often called perch bugs, they are gotten from muddy stream bottoms by digging and screening. These and similar baits can be kept in screened boxes filled with three or four inches of mud and submerged in water at about the same temperatures of the location from which they were originally taken. They will eat each other, however, unless fed chopped worms and small insects. The stonefly must be kept in water as cool as the stream from which it came. Place these insects in a container with rocks and slime from the same general location of capture. Do the same for mayfly nymphs and caddis larvae. These last build the sand and refuse cases in which they live. They won't keep long, only a few hours, unless in very cool and aerated water. They can be baited dead, however.

When wading or walking along a stream and fishing, the bait storage box or can should be deposited in shallow water, the fisherman returning to it for bait replenishment. Only a short supply of baits should be carried in the belt bait can.

OTHER AQUATIC BAITS

The crayfish is one of the most versatile aquatic baits for all game fish. They are found in profusion along the shores of most lakes and slow rivers and can be seen easily at night by flashlight in rocks, grass, weeds and along the shore. Use a small dip net, but be quick about it! They can dart right back into the water before one has a chance to dump them into the minnow bucket or similar container. They are anti-social with regard to fellow crayfish, and they will kill each other unless given a piece of meat or fish to divert their attention.

Keep them in cool water similar to their natural habitat. A large container with a few rocks, some gravel and a good

CATCHING, KEEPING AND CARRYING LIVE BAIT

supply of weeds or grass from the lake is preferred. If they are to be kept only a short time, snip off their claws (they are fished without them anyway). This will help preserve them longer in usable condition.

The little stone catfish is another favorite, especially with bass, walleye and pike fishermen. It grows to about a four-inch length and is found under stones and stream bed debris or in lake shallows where one can wade easily and, with flashlight in hand, spot them among the weeds. They are quite hardy and live longer than minnows if kept cool in frequently-changed water. Feed them small bits of meat or dead fish. They are better fished alive though dead casts will catch fish, too, and are preferred by many anglers. As suggested, keep the basic supply in the stream or lake near the fishing area and use it for replenishing the belt bait holder. When fishing from a boat, take them along in a large bait can.

LIVE MINNOWS

These are most generally taken in seine nets, baited minnow traps (bought at the tackle store), baited dip nets and occasionally by angling. When angling, use very thin nylon line, a tiny hook about size eighteen and short shanked, and a small bit of worm. The larger minnows can be caught this way and such size is desirable for big bass, pike and musky fishing. Some minnows keep well in aquariums and tanks (a clean garbage can is good where there is slow running water from a garden hose). They can also be kept in a screened box placed underwater in the lake or stream being fished.

Again, a short supply is carried in the belt bait holder, and replenished with fresh water every few minutes. Don't try to cram too many minnows into the small container. It is better to make more trips to the supply than to fish with dead or near-dead minnows. In the back of the book is a "dictionary" of live bait types; from this one may discover some "native" to his particular locality. Incidentally, some of these fish are quite attractive and it just might be that one could use a home aquarium container for such bait storage.

Caution: *Never* use carp or goldfish as bait. They are illegal in most states and harmful if introduced into lakes and streams.

LAND-BRED INSECTS

Grasshoppers, crickets, and beetles are among the easiest to find and catch and they are excellent baits for panfish and trout. They're easy to bait up due to the hard shells and thorax into which the hook is inserted.

Grasshoppers are best caught at dawn when the dew is still on the ground and the insects are still somewhat quiet. Same for crickets, although many of these can be caught at night under the porch light. They will stay alive for at least twenty-four hours if kept in a container with adequate air vents. During the day keep them in the shade and as cool as possible. Include some grass and leaves for their protection and food.

Moths, millers and large flying bugs and insects can be used for bait, too. These will die quickly, but they can be used on light leaders and small hooks for panfish and trout. They are fished "dry-fly" style on a long leader and impaled on a very small hook. Keep them in a bottle or box and, if wearing a fishing creel, place the box in a creel where it is easily available.

Unnatural baits such as beef, pork and cheese should be wrapped in aluminum foil and kept out of the sun and heat.

9

Freshwater Fishing Accessories

THE FRESHWATER ANGLER, stream wader, lakeshore walker or boat fisherman must have a reasonable amount of adequate and proper equipment. However, he will find that only a modest amount of the equipment offered in tackle and sporting goods stores is really essential to bait fishing.

Consider the little barefoot boy; sapling pole, store line and a hook. He will catch fish, that's for sure! But, as circumstances warrant and as he grows older, he'll eventually need boot-foot waders for lakeshore and small stream wading; chest-high waders for big stream and deep-lake wading. He will need landing nets—a short one for wading and a long-handled one for boat fishing. Clothes will be chosen according to temperature and season; this goes for rain gear, too. Outdoor exposure requires insect repellent; a small first aid kit for cuts, bruises and bites; a plastic bag for carrying food while wading; a lunchbox or large ice chest for long trips in the car or boat and finally, a big tackle box for tools, terminal tackle, reels, hook hones and flashlight.

A fish stringer will be needed if the catch is to be kept alive. A good sharp hunting knife, or a combination jackknife with can opener, screwdriver and punch are also recommended. A waterproof match container, glasses case and similar accessories are definite musts.

Actual fishing accessories include a thermometer (the barometer can be kept at home or in camp), protective sunglasses for glarefree days and best vision when staring into water, and a cap with a broad visor to shelter the face and eyes.

Several combinations of bait containers suitable for ready transportation and stock use are needed ashore or afloat.

BOATING FISHERMAN

For the boating fisherman, the required size and relative seaworthiness of his craft varies according to the need. A cartop rowboat, canoe or square-end pram are all that is necessary for small ponds, lakes and rivers where the wind doesn't churn up dangerous situations. Canoes, kayaks, and even inflatable rubber or fabric boats are ideal for many of the smaller streams.

In general, the boat should be able to handle two anglers at least, and possibly three, complete with the weight of gear taken aboard. The motor must work without flaw; be neither too powerful and heavy nor lacking in the huskiness needed

FRESHWATER FISHING ACCESSORIES

to bring the fisherman home in a hurry when conditions dictate. These combinations are best found by noting the rigs already on the lake or river to be fished, or by consultation with a reliable boat and motor dealer who handles top-grade equipment. Lights when necessary, life jackets or preserver cushions are musts for all those aboard. The same applies to a strong anchor rope and anchor capable of holding the boat in strong current or wind, plus a spare anchor and rope supply for emergency situations. A mechanic's kit for motor repairs; a spare can for gas and oil; a good pair of oars and oarlocks or paddles; a pole, chain and lock for boat and motor. Additions will include extra cushions, seatbacks, rod holders, bow wheel and motor controls, windshield, canvas top and radio. A bailing can is also a must, plus sponges and rags for cleaning after the trip.

A built-in bait box under the center seat or under the bow cover is quite advisable unless bait is to be carried in a separate container. A piece of canvas or tarp can be used to cover the bait box, food containers and extra clothes to protect them from rain, spray or excessive heat. There's more to come, depending on the fisherman's needs, desires and the size of his pocketbook.

PART III
SALTWATER BAIT FISHING

10

Tides, Tackle and Bait

SALTWATER BAIT FISHING can be divided into three basic categories. It is done from the shore, casting from the beach, rocks, jetties and mudflats. Casting, trolling and stillfishing are done from boats in protected bays and inlets, outlets, inland waterways and coves. Offshore trolling is done on the open ocean, near the oceanic shelves, drop-offs, reefs and islands.

One does not need to own a boat. There are party boats, where as many as a hundred anglers join together for half-day, or full-day trips to the fishing grounds. Take one of these excursions and anglers will be seen fishing with varied types of equipment and using many diversified techniques for catching fish. Small boats and motors can be rented for bay fishing. More expensive craft can be "chartered" complete with captain and first mate for a trip offshore in search of the big prizes. Generally four to six anglers can chip in and charter one of these boats for half-day, full-day or as long as desired, all depending on what vacation time and wallet permit. In party boats and charter boats, the bait and—in some instances—the tackle is supplied, including guidance on how to use them by the crew. This is, incidentally, often compulsory since the reputation of the boat and crew depends upon their patrons catching fish, hence they wish to maintain their image as guides "par excellence."

TIDES

Perhaps the biggest natural difference found in the ocean that does not exist in lakes or most rivers, is the tide. Every six hours the ocean's water "rises" and every six hours it "falls." In some areas like the Bay of Fundy between Upper Maine and New Brunswick, the tide rises more than forty feet—quite a change! In other parts of the world such as in the Bahamas, the change amounts to only a few feet.

This constant action keeps life in the ocean moving in a continually predictable routine. The fisherman who knows the schedule of natural events can plan his strategy accordingly and, depending on fish migrations and the movement of baitfish, be assured of catching enough fish to fill his freezer.

This tidal action affects everything from the amount of water to the minutest form of life, including the bait upon which the resident or roving fish feed. As the tide comes into a bay, for example, clams, worms and other forms of food

A simple rowboat, outboard open boat, limited offshore skiff, party boat, and charter boat show the variety of craft used in saltwater angling.

TIDES, TACKLE AND BAIT

liven up. The minnows begin to feed and form schools. The bigger fish move in from deeper water searching for them. When the tide is on the rise, it is a good time to fish, particularly near the "top" of the tide. But in many cases an equally good time can be had on the "ebb" of the tide. Thus, when the current is falling, it brings the baitfish down out of the inlets and away from the coves and into the channels. Big fish know this and wait there for them. Learn the subtleties of tide action in relation to the wind and its effect on bait and sport fish.

TACKLE
Reels

Selection of the proper saltwater reel is relatively simple since needs are well categorized. Standard code numbers designate reel sizes which range from 1/0 to 6/0 inclusive; the large sizes from 9/0 to 16/0. Capacity varies due to line sizes; a 1/0 will hold 225 yards of 20-pound dacron or 350 yards in monofilament, for example.

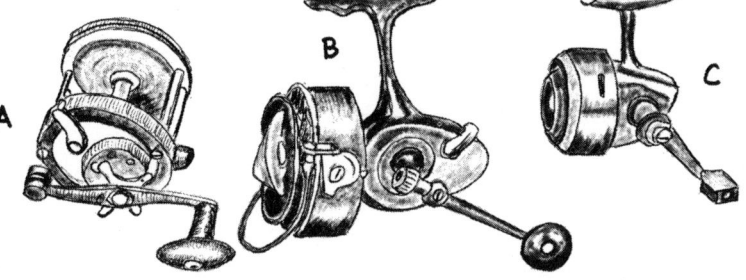

Most common reels for saltwater bait fishing: A—A typical revolving-spool reel; B—A typical open-face spinning reel; C—A closed-face spinning reel which is most versatile and may be mounted above or below the rod handle on the conventional baitcasting rod.

Saltwater Fishing Lines

A few years ago, the most popular lines were made from Irish or Belgian linen; braided and twisted, it was known as "cuttyhunk." Linen lines were graded according to thread numbers from 3 to 72; thread strength, three pounds, wet, a 54-thread line testing at 162 pounds. These lines and designations are still used in tournament fishing. Today, most lines are braided nylon or dacron while some, including the spincasters, prefer monofilament. Braided nylon lines are rated to pound test, but not according to threads; they are available in spools of 50 to 100 yards, in boxes of from two to six spools. In the same sizes they come packed up to 1200 yards and in a variety of colors. Monofilament lines run from 6 to 50-pound test for saltwater fishing.

Wire lines of stainless steel, bronze-copper and other corrosive-proof metals are used with Monel, the present favorite for deep offshore trolling. Made in twist, braid and some fabricovered lead-core versions, they range in strength from five to 85 pounds.

BAITS FOR SALTWATER PANFISH

It is advisable to start with small fish that abound in or near shore where they can be reached by fishing from a dock, or a small rowboat. The tackle requirements are few: a hand line, some hooks and a sinker and a bucket of clams are sufficient to catch flounders, porgy, small blackfish, small grouper and a veritable host of other small fish that defy listing. Throw the line overboard and any one of fifty species of fish may grab for the bait. There are certain groups of fish that are commonly found in specific locations, however. The

TIDES, TACKLE AND BAIT

flounder, for instance, is found in sandy-muddy bottoms where clams and sea worms abound. The porgy is found in deeper water and can be taken on cut bait the same as blackfish, grouper, yellowtail, and redfish. Weakfish are best taken on live or rigged minnows and a southern cousin, the spotted sea trout, is best caught on live shrimp. Pompano will take cut bait, but their favorites are shrimp, and shelled sand fleas.

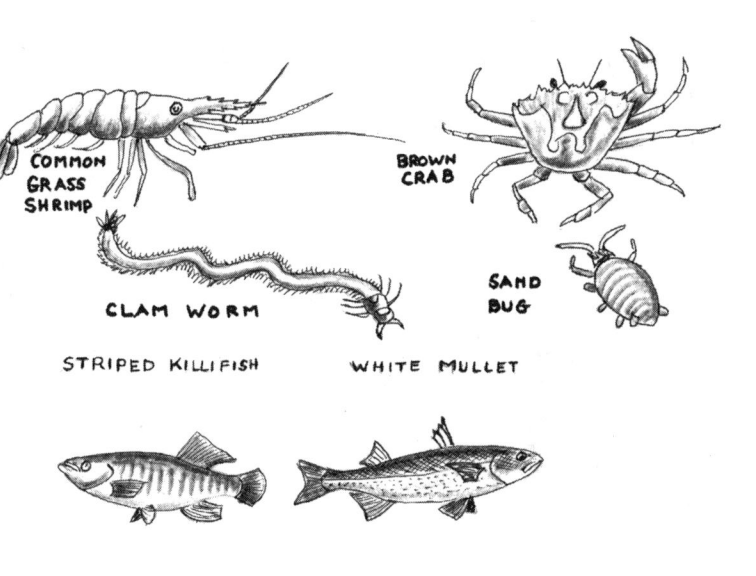

These are readily available natural baits for most saltwater panfish. Dockside bait dealers, tackle stores and local guides can obtain these or the fisherman can gather them from local waters.

NATURAL SALTWATER BAITS AND HOW TO RIG THEM

Sea Worms and Rigs

Sea worms are the saltwater counterpart to earthworms used in freshwater fishing. All but the largest offshore monsters feed on them at one time or another. The sand worms, also called clam worms, are native to the East Coast and are called musselworms (pileworms on the West Coast). They are easily found in mudflats, sand and shell bottoms, around old pilings and barnacled rocks. They average from five to twelve inches in length. The muck or bloodworm is another old standby. Found in the same general locations, it can also be unearthed in mudflats. Keep these worms alive for days by putting them in the shade in a well-aired box with seaweed and rock moss. Separate them or they tend to ball up and die quickly. An excellent bottom fishing bait, these are used extensively for trolling for striped bass; they'll also take weakfish, croakers, porgies, corbina, and the like.

Clams and Similar Shellfish on the Hook

The surf clam, or sea clam "skimmer" is one of the most widely used followed by the ordinary hardshell. *Any* clam or mussel will take all manner of fish except big game and in all fishing methods. (They are also very good to eat raw when the fishing becomes dull.) Keep them on ice or in a cool container, giving them new water every few hours.

Squid Bait and Rigs

Many species of squid are found on both coasts. If one is lucky, he can find them right after a high tide on the beach

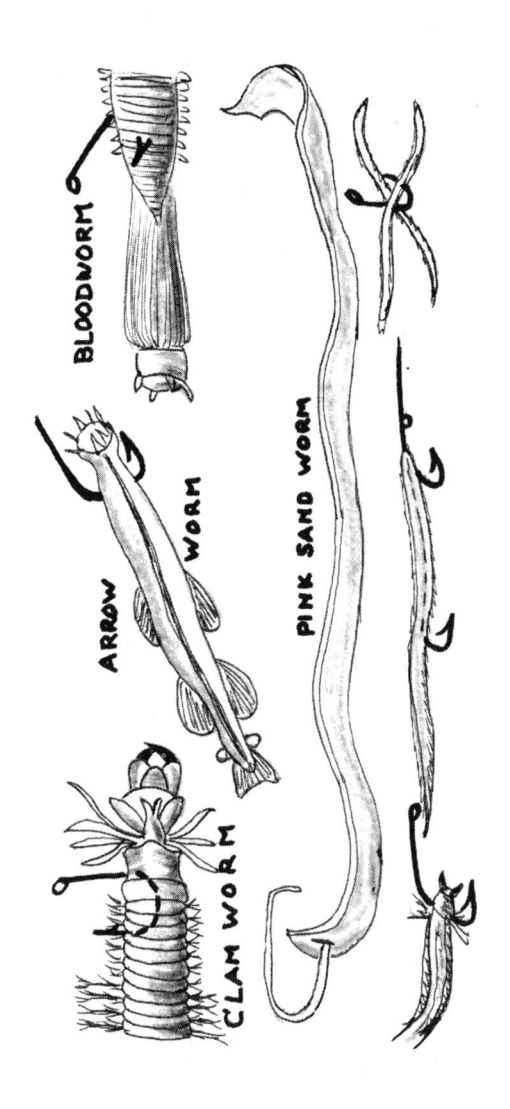

The common and most available sea worms and suggested rigs for various types of fishing.

COMMON SOFT SHELL

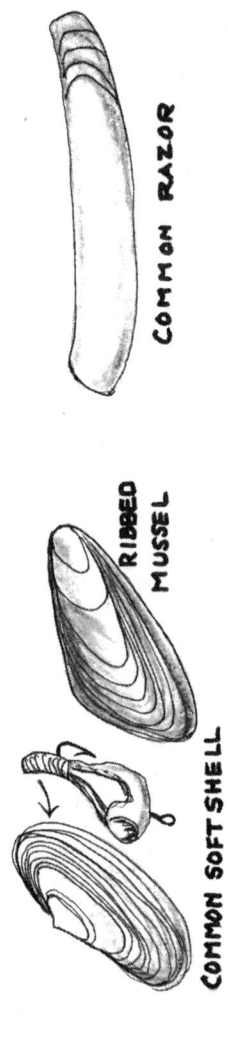

RIBBED MUSSEL

COMMON RAZOR

Clams suffice for most inshore bottom fishing and are also used in some dock, jetty and beach fishing. Note (figures at left) how to rig them.

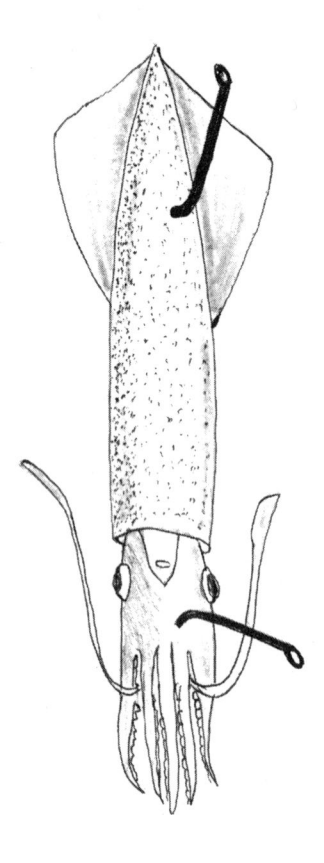

Squid are used in many forms of saltwater fishing and are good baits at all depths. Rig them as shown.

or trapped in pools of shallow water after the tide has receded. Fish markets, tackle stores and waterside marinas have them in season. Squid can be rigged whole or in parts. The large-size whole squid is a preferred bait for offshore fishing.

Crabs for Bottom Baiting

Most bay, beach and inshore deep stillfishermen use live crabs as effective bait. When taken by net, trap or bought at the bait store, they are best when in the soft-shell period. Claws are removed when put on the hook. The most popular and common is the blue crab. The calico or lady crab found on the beaches is logically a favored one for surf fishing. Fiddler crabs are most popular with bottom stillfishermen, especially when seeking blackfish, weakfish, channel bass, striped bass and (when they are in-shore) bluefish and pollock.

Shrimp Baits and Hooking

The most popular bait in southern waters is the shrimp, either jumbo or the common smaller "grass" variety. They can be kept alive in a box loaded with seaweed and watered occasionally. When off shore, keep them in a live bait pail and give them fresh water often.

Baitfish and Rigs

A long list of species abounds on both coasts, and they can be caught by netting or trapping. They can also be bought from bait dealers, kept on ice or alive in bait buckets. Herring, mullet, menhaden (mossbunker) are the most popular.

Crabs can be cast, but usually they are used for inshore stillfishing. Rig as shown.

Shrimp is a popular bait in southern waters for all but the large deep-sea fish. Rig as shown.

TIDES, TACKLE AND BAIT

143

Pilcher, alewife, and sardines are also favorites for both inshore and offshore angling. For small game fish and bottom feeders, the easily caught killifish and the more delicate speering, or silversides, are tops. Fish them live, if possible.

The common eel is another favorite, though it usually is considered best for night fishing for striped bass, bluefish and the like.

Baitfish are used in many ways, in stillfishing, casting and trolling. This shows how to rig them for whichever purpose.

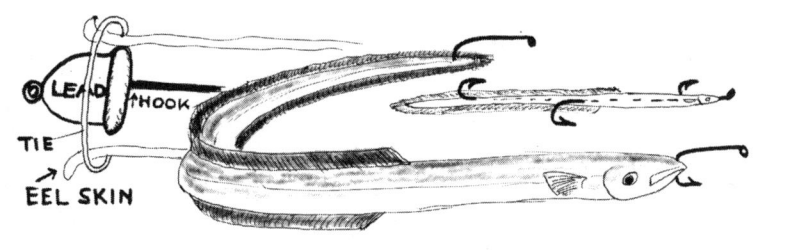

Kept frozen for rigging or alive for better action, the common eel, when available, is rigged in various ways as shown.

SALTWATER LINES AND TERMINAL TACKLE

Armed with a simple hand line or a light boat rod, or a light-to-medium spinning rod, the fisherman can "bottom fish" for these and others with a simple rig or two designed merely to get the bait down to the bottom for stillfishing and to hold it deep in current or ocean tide. Little or no casting is needed, since the bait will drop directly down anyway to be dragged along on or near the bottom by action of the current.

While some of the fish have soft mouths, others have very sharp teeth, so it is advisable to use either very heavy nylon leaders or, for the bigger fish, the plastic-coated metal ones. The choice of hook size should be made on the spot. The place for one to buy hooks is where he buys bait, for the local "salts" know the best rigs for their territory and the most commonly taken fish species.

SPECIAL KNOTS FOR SALTWATER FISHERMEN

These are special knots in addition to those elsewhere shown that are used mostly by saltwater anglers. These include the blood knot, leader knot, perfection loop, end loop, dropper, jam, tucked sheet bend, clinch, lark's head, double eye, and key loop. To become adept at tying these, practice in the dark, so if the time ever comes "out there" they can be tied quickly.

LEADERS FOR SALTWATER BAIT FISHING

Leaders are a convenience when quick changes of terminal gear are necessary. Short wire leaders, 6 to 9 inches long, al-

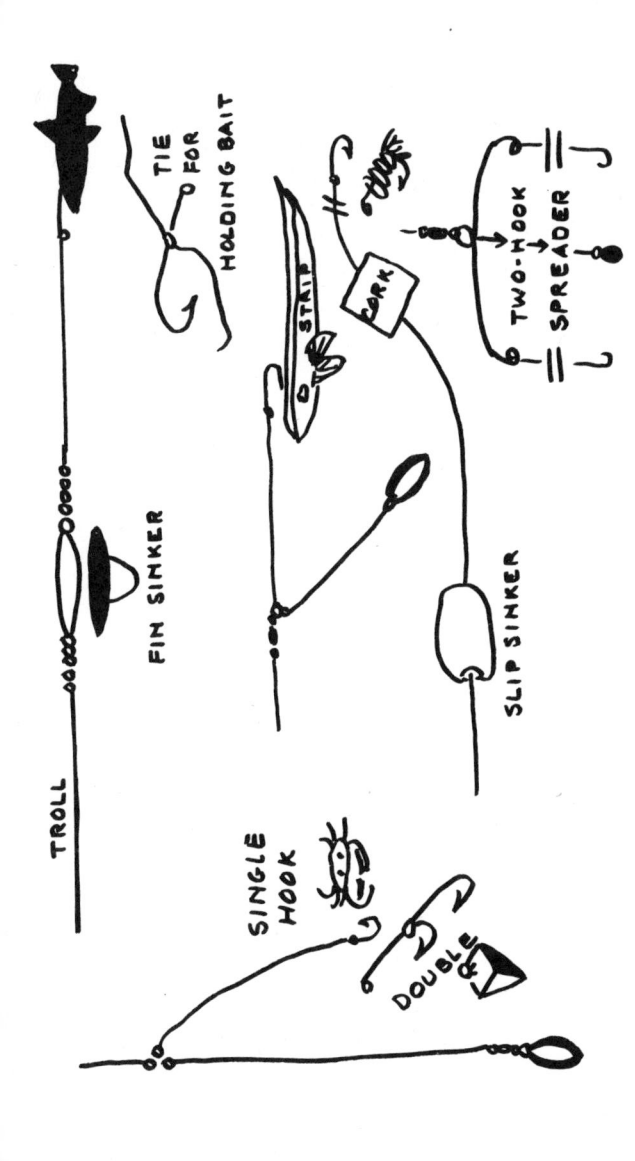

Here are general rigs for most saltwater angling. The fisherman should be able to make up all combinations, making sure that when he goes fishing he has a good supply.

PERFECTION LOOP KNOT

DROPPER SNELL KNOT

LOOP KNOT

JAM KNOT

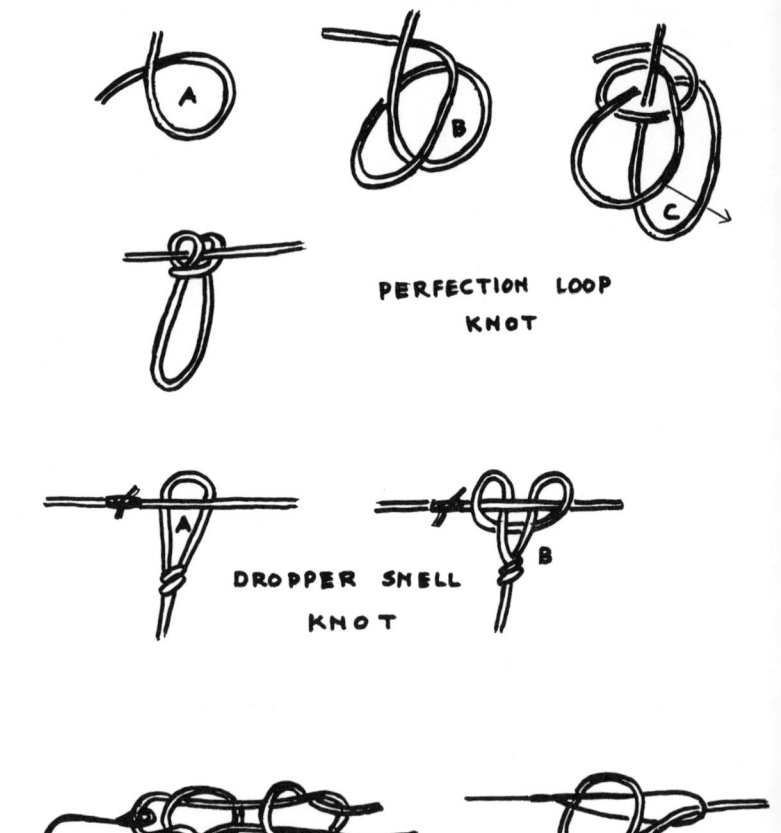

Tying new knots seems difficult at first; one feels "all thumbs." But after a few trials, it all becomes simple. And, learn to tie them so well it can be done in the dark. Here are some very useful ones.

FISHERMAN'S BEND

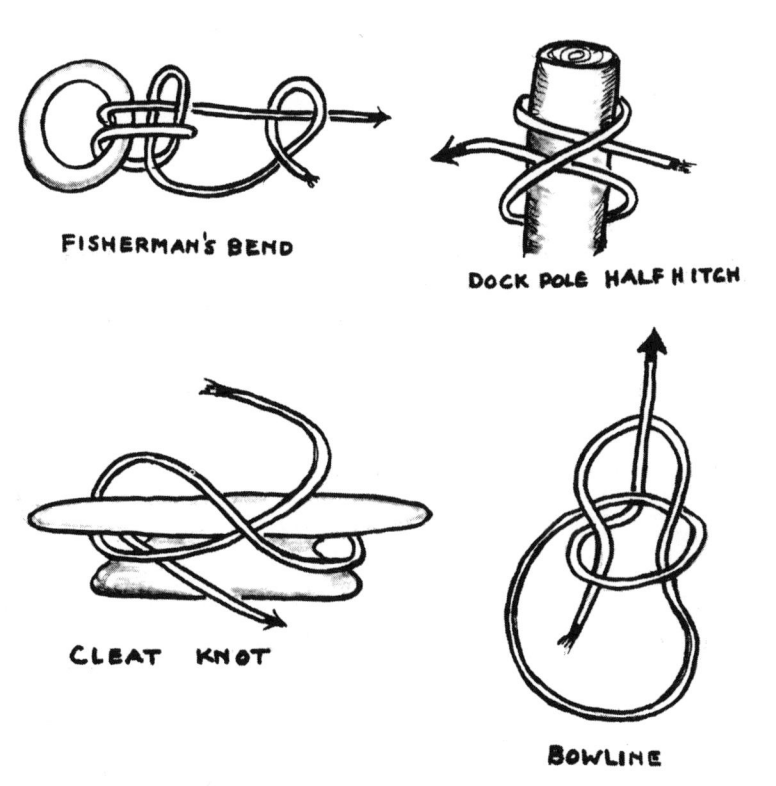

DOCK POLE HALF HITCH

CLEAT KNOT

BOWLINE

In learning to tie new knots, start with a fairly thick line. Here are some more knots very useful to fishermen and boaters.

ready made up, look like those in the illustration; the single-strand wire leader and the braided version that is sometimes covered with plastic. For light spinning, the 9 to 12-inch length is better and for trolling, use one up to three feet for in-shore purposes and longer ones up to fifteen feet for billfish.

While leaders are packaged in almost limitless variety, many anglers prefer to make up their own. Sizes range from number 2 in stainless steel testing at 27 pounds (30 in wire) all the way up to number 14 testing at 265 pounds in wire.

Single-strand monofilament leader material comes from 5X designation testing at 1.25 pounds, to 0/5 at from 20 to 60 pounds. Casting conditions limit the length, but trolling leaders can be any practical length desired. They are attached to the line by snap swivels, or tied in as the knots show in the illustrations.

SINKERS FOR SALTWATER FISHING

Lead sinkers are produced in various shapes and weights for the necessary balance and use required. The main purpose of the sinker is to get the bait to the bottom and, when desired, keep it there despite boat drift, current or tide. It is also used in trolling to maintain the bait at a certain, desired depth. Several terminal rigs are needed in combination with the right sinker and the important bait type.

One of the most popular is the bank sinker; good for all-round use in both fresh and salt water. The diamond sinkers are preferred for bottom fishing in deep, currented waters. The square sinker is suggested for fishing over broken and rocky ocean floors and current-ripped bays and inlets, for it tends to ride over the rocks instead of becoming easily

SINGLE WIRE

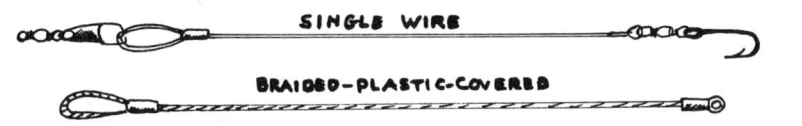

BRAIDED-PLASTIC-COVERED

These are typical examples of wire leaders already made up for swivels and snaps. They can be made up easily enough at home or they are available in various lengths and fittings at tackle stores. The wise fisherman should always have a good supply.

snagged. The egg-shaped sinker, used extensively in freshwater fishing, is called the slip sinker, since the hole through the weight allows the line to pass through, offering free action to the bait and a free run to the fish. The pyramid sinkers are used for both bottom and surf fishing. They are particularly popular with surf fishermen fishing from sandy beaches. The pyramid sinks in the sand readily, and its flat edge dredges up sand as it is pulled along, this burying the sinker in the sand. Trolling weights are built along entirely different requirements and although any weight that will not twist the line can be used, specially designed ones are preferred.

HOOKS FOR SALTWATER BAITS

Don't minimize the importance of using the right hook just from looking at the illustrations and thinking they all look alike. The right bait has been chosen, gathered and prepared with care. Now, put it on the right hook against the need of the moment. Buy a good supply of hooks and keep them dry and sharp. In the case of the bigger hooks designed for saltwater use, it is better to file them down from the relatively

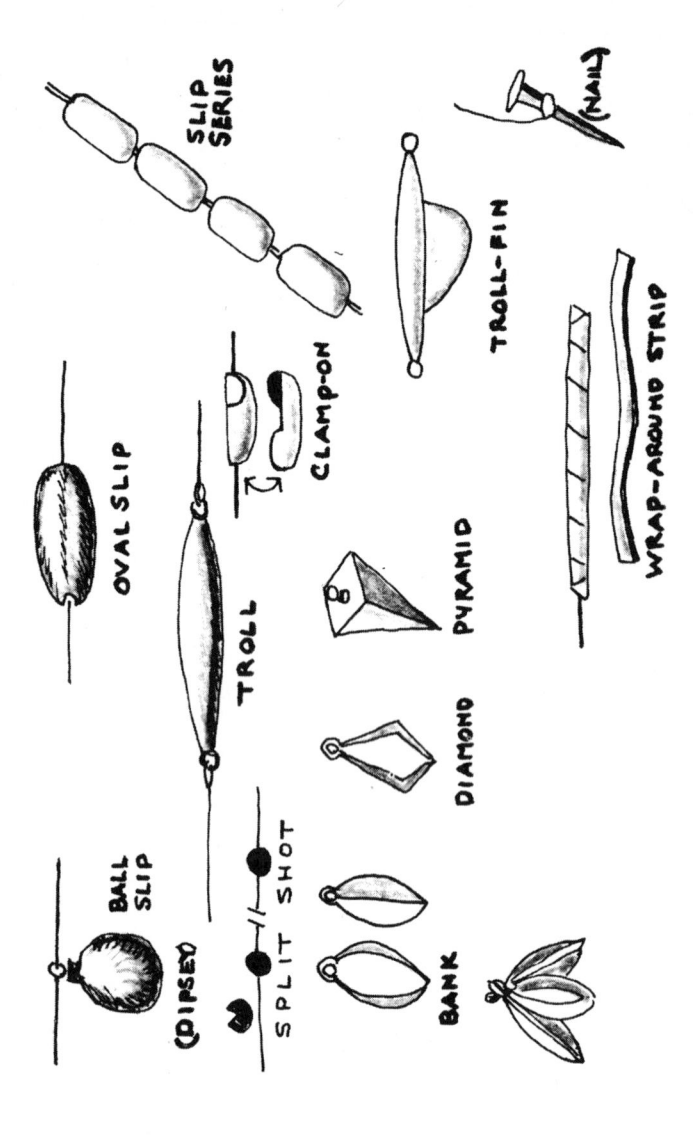

Sinkers for saltwater angling use are varied in shape and weight. Note these styles and their uses in relation to baits to be used and the kind of fishing to be involved.

TIDES, TACKLE AND BAIT

dull point produced at the factory. By contrast, the wire freshwater hooks usually come with very sharp points and barbs.

Hooks for freshwater fishing are limited to a relatively few styles and it doesn't matter too much if a "wrong" hook is used unless it is too light or small to handle the fish. Saltwater hooks, however, are chosen for their power and ability to hold various kinds of bait and securely hook and hold strong fighting fish. The fisherman should check at the local bait and tackle store where he'll be fishing, especially if the area and species of fish are new to him. "Old salt" local knowhow is a great aid in hook selection.

Shown here are the common hook points, hook shapes and sizes of hooks used for small fresh and saltwater fishing. The specially designed O'Shaughnessy patterns are "musts" for the larger fish up to and including sharks.

In general, the sproat has a wide angle of penetration and it is used for mackerel, kingfish, haddock, cod and small striped bass. The limerick, with its half-round bend, is for bottom fish such as cod, haddock and grouper. The Aberdeen is used for its wide gap for small baits in fishing for croakers, weakfish and the like. The Siwash is used primarily for Pacific salmon though it is popular now in the East for fish that are surface-active, such as bluefish, striped bass and dolphin.

The Carlisle is a round bend for flounders, blues and fluke. The Chestertown is the favorite of some flounder fishermen and the Eagle Claw is best for all bottom fish. The O'Shaughnessy is similar to the sproat and limerick, but made of very heavy wire. The Virginia is known as the "short bite" hook for sheepshead, blackfish or any others with bony mouths and very sharp teeth. The Kirby is a favorite with sucking fishes such as ling, cod, kingfish, whitefish, etc.

Big-game hooks are specially forged with very round bends and sometimes offset barbs for sailfish.

All hooks can be snelled onto either nylon monofilament or wire leaders. Double and treble hooks are also used in salt water, but basically on artificial lures.

The biggest hooks of all are made for sharks; these run as long as 12 inches and are four to five inches across at the gap. They are not attached to conventional leaders, but to chains up to six feet long.

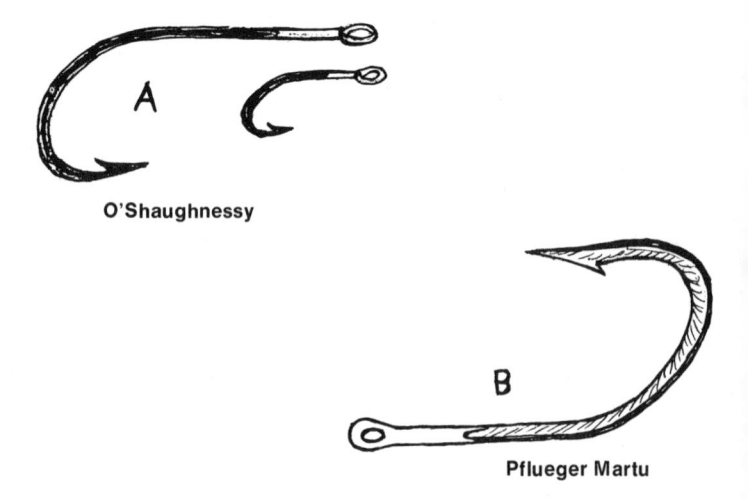

O'Shaughnessy

Pflueger Martu

Study these various hook designs and keep them in mind when shopping for hooks. Keep hooks in dry containers and preferably hooked into corks or in segmented boxes so they don't become mixed up. (Not shown in actual size—illustrated as to kind or type only.)

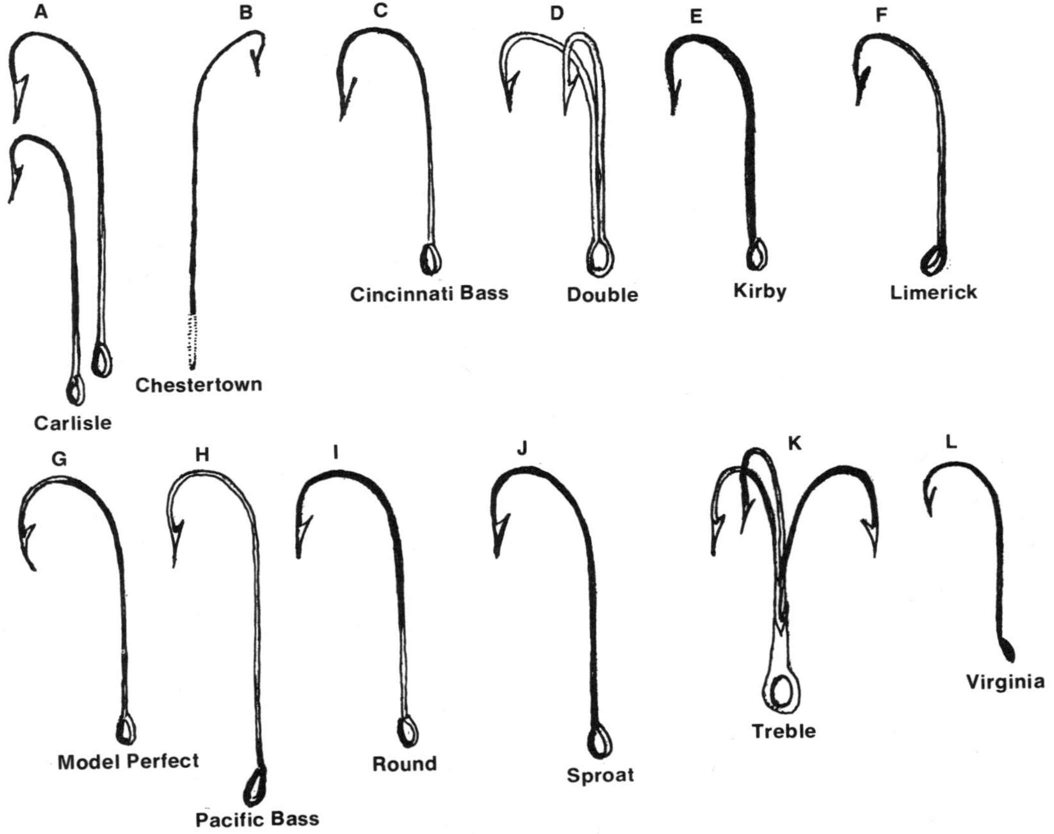
A
B
C
D
E
F
Cincinnati Bass
Double
Kirby
Limerick
Chestertown
Carlisle
G
H
I
J
K
L
Virginia
Treble
Model Perfect
Round
Sproat
Pacific Bass

RODS

Trolling Rods

These are classified according to tip weight; a four-ounce tip usually five feet in length; 17-inch butt is in the light-tackle classification. Tips running through four-ounces, six ounces, nine-ounces and twelve-ounces lead into the medium-weight class. These and the heavier classifications have pulley tip-rollers on the tip-top rather than the simple ring guide. Boat rods are also used for trolling; the shorter surf rods will also suffice, although the long butt is more difficult to handle unless the angler stands. With the heavy freshwater and medium saltwater boat rods usually used for bottom fishing, limited casting can also be done. For extremely light saltwater work, conventional freshwater spinning and baitcasting tackle can be used for trolling, stillfishing and casting, if light weights are used and long casts are not required.

TYPICAL 6 FT. ONE-PIECE WITH FIVE GUIDES AND TIP-TOP

A typical saltwater trolling rod. They vary from the largest and heaviest for big game offshore fishing to smallboat rods for inshore rowboat angling.

Stillfishing Rods

Bottom fishermen like the tubular solid-glass, so-called "boat rod", with one or two sections in lengths of from five to six

TIDES, TACKLE AND BAIT

feet. They are also used for light and medium trolling. For shallow bay and inland waterways, fishing for weakfish, flounder, two to four-ounce rods are recommended.

BOAT-STILL-FISHING ROD WITH RUBBER BUTT CAP   FIVE (PLUS) FT. ONE-PIECE

The stillfishing rod is a most versatile one; here's a standard type.

Baitcasting Rods

Freshwater baitcasting rods with reel seats able to accommodate standard fresh and light saltwater reels are used for all types of light ocean fishing and casting. Lengths from five to six-and-one-half feet are good for general work. A reel taking 150 yards of ten-pound line is about right for most situations.

OFF-SET HANDLE LIGHT BAIT-CASTING TWO-PIECE ROD

The baitcasting rod conventional to freshwater or saltwater fishing. It can be used with the regular baitcasting reel or a closed-face spinning or spincasting reel.

Spinning Rods

These range from ultra-light freshwater (for catching bait and good for snapper blues and small dockside fish) to the longest and stoutest surf and trolling rods with matching reels.

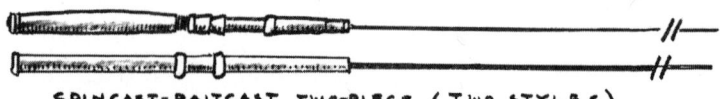

SPINCAST-BAITCAST TWO-PIECE (TWO STYLES)

Typical spinning rod with large guides, designed for open-face reels. If necessary, it can be used with all reel types.

STILLFISHING TECHNIQUES

Fishing can be done from a bridge, dock, point of rocks, or from a rowboat. Go out to the fishing area "on the tide" and join other anglers seeking the same species. Watch them; take up a strategic position by noting current drift or tide force; rig up with the proper terminal tackle and bait; throw it in and feed line out until it hits bottom; then pull the bait up sharply to a height of about two feet from mud, or three feet above a rock or weed bottom. There are many bottom fish that are bait stealers; fish most would not want to keep if they hooked them. The bait should be kept above snags. The fisherman will get to know the "feel" when something other than a preferred species starts nibbling and fooling around down there. Inspect the bait regularly. Upon any solid pull of the line, haul it in. There is a certain special sensitivity in this kind of fishing to become acquainted with that will stand one in good stead for bigger prizes.

Move the line up and down constantly a foot or two, to give the bait a sense of life. This also helps one develop a feel for the "take" of a good fish.

Spotted sea trout are caught with live shrimp. Using the bobber adjusted to the depth required, the bait will remain above the bottom. Allow it to wave in the current.

TIDES, TACKLE AND BAIT   157

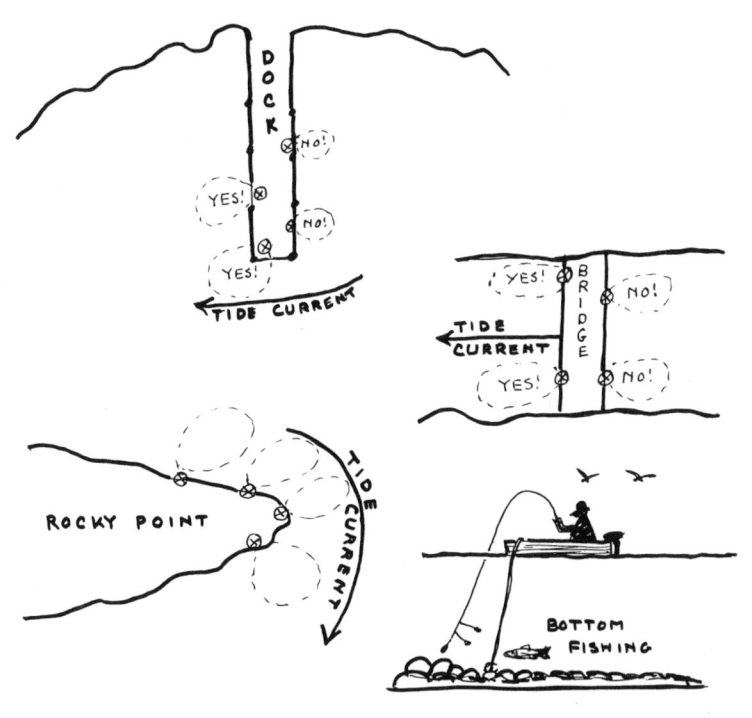

Some common saltwater fishing situations. Take advantage of the tidal currents (see "Yes" and "No" notations).

TROLLING TECHNIQUES

Trolling and certain drift fishing is effective for weakfish or sea trout, jacks, redfish and a host of other worthy fishes. Drifting along on the current, one can cover much more territory than the anchored fisherman, and be apt to encounter

158   INTRODUCTION TO BAIT FISHING

more varied fish species. The trolling rig is a mere variation of the bottom rig of conventional terminal tackle. Use enough swivels and check for weeds, or else the line will tangle unmercifully. Don't try to work line that's too long; 100 feet is enough. Try to hold the boat in a nearly sta-

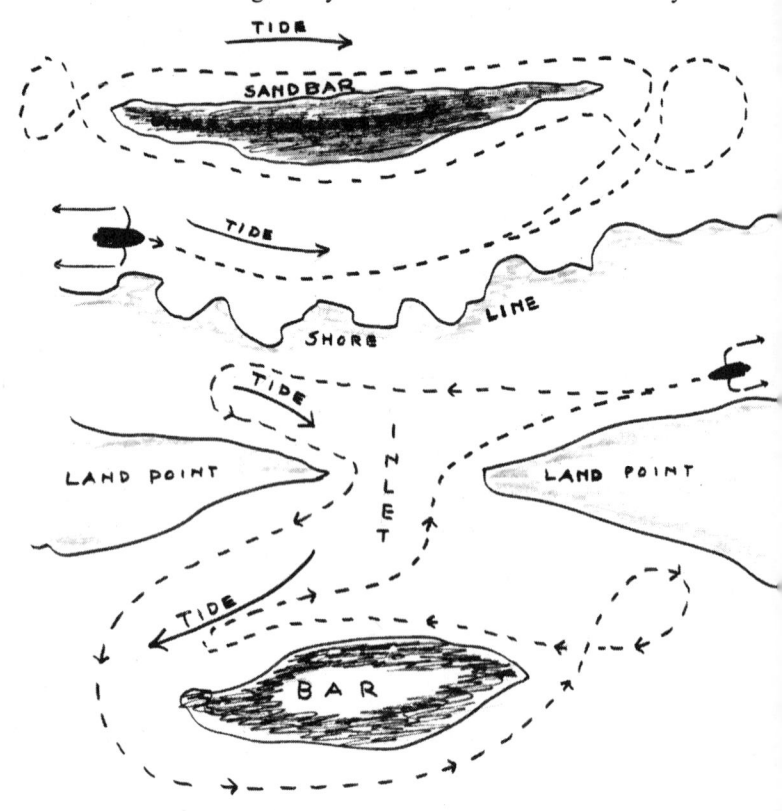

Illustrating a couple of suggested trolling courses in circumstances common to inshore saltwater fishing.

tionary position in the tide; allow the current to do the actual trolling. At other times, drift with the current and the line will actually be "stillfished" while moving along.

In the case of casting live shrimp or cut bait, one can cast ahead of his drift; allow the baits to sink and the bobber to float the works along a mangrove shore or edge of rocks, varying boat speed and position to the current and size of area being fished.

Most bottom fish dislike strong current. A good trolling time to pick is the slack of the tide, or just as the tide hits the low or begins the rise, or just before and immediately after high tide. The high is generally the better of the two, and far superior to a "running tide" for this kind of fishing. When the tide is flowing fast, drift and troll with it. Work the points of land, rocky ledges and reefs, yes—but don't neglect the sandy bays and especially the muddy sections, particularly if fishing for flounders. Go aboard for a day's trip on a party boat. It is quite educational.

11
Surf, Beach and Jetty Fishing

ONE ACTIVE STEP up from fishing for the little bottom fish of bays and coves is the sport of jetty, surf and beach fishing; casting and trolling for the more energetic varieties. Bluefish up to ten pounds can be and are taken from these vantages. They come in with the tide, rushing schools of bait. As they surge by and spot cut bait, they'll hit it. Same for striped bass, pollock, jacks, mackerel, snook and tarpon, not to mention channel bass, shark and many more species. In between these runs—nothing but bait-stealers. Sometimes one will fish almost an entire tide and enjoy peak fishing only for a matter of a few minutes. It's a waiting game, but well worth it.

Tide and wind are the prime considerations. When the

SURF, BEACH AND JETTY FISHING

fish are "in", the best times for jetty and beach fishing are at the up-turn of the tide from low, and again at high to an hour or so after, night or day. Consider the wind direction and try to locate a position for casting with the wind rather than against it.

For the smaller fish, use cut bait, clams, sea worms and crabs, but when the stripers and blues are in, for example, whole baitfish or crabs that can be cast a good distance are best.

If these cannot be acquired, cut bait will still suffice. Whole or cut squid are often used by night fishermen as are eel skins attached to specially weighted hook rigs. These last are good for fishing canals or in fishing from bridges and jetties.

For the surf, whole baitfish, squid, shrimp or any cut bait such as clams, strips of flesh from caught fish, etc., will be quite sufficient.

Wind direction and force may be much against the fisherman. If so, he may find himself up against the old problem of trying to figure out how to get the heavy bait a good distance out and away from him without having the wind drop it near his feet. Therefore, never go under-tackled for this sport; conditions under which casting may have to be done coupled with the potential power of a hooked fish suggest the angler should rather go over-tackled than under. A big bluefish, tarpon or striper can give more than the fisherman bargained for. Learn to cast with accuracy and as far out as possible without line snags and hang-ups. Bring a lot of terminal tackle since bottom snags will happen often, and also be sure to bring an oversupply of bait.

The bait should be kept frozen and in a container that will preserve it as long as possible. Keep it out of the sun. If live bait is used, sink the bait can or cage underwater, tie it securely to a rock and watch the tide level. Watch the relationship between wind, tide and barometer, keeping alert for quick changes.

Depending on the season, dress accordingly. The night fisherman should make sure everything is in its right place, available by touch. Again, keep an eye on the weather. It would be a shame to miss good fishing just because of forgetting to bring the proper clothing, food or other necessities.

TERMINAL TACKLE FOR BEACH AND JETTY

In addition to the recommended terminal tackle for general and bottom fishing, the fisherman should use heavier gear and preferably metal leaders with casting rods of strength. The choice of sinker styles and weights depends upon the bottom conditions of the fishing locale. The diamond sinker, for example is better for the sandy bottoms because it digs into the sand faster than a round weight. However, the round weight will not slide along bottom muck and mud as quickly as will the diamond. These are seemingly small details but after one has fished awhile, he'll realize the importance of correct tackle, correct down to the last detail. Recommended here are the standards, but it is most advisable to follow the advice of a local tackle dealer and tips from other anglers familiar with the particular fishing grounds involved.

TROLLING BEACH AND JETTY

It would seem better to be out in a boat for fishing a jetty or beach with more efficiency. Over the years, however, one will

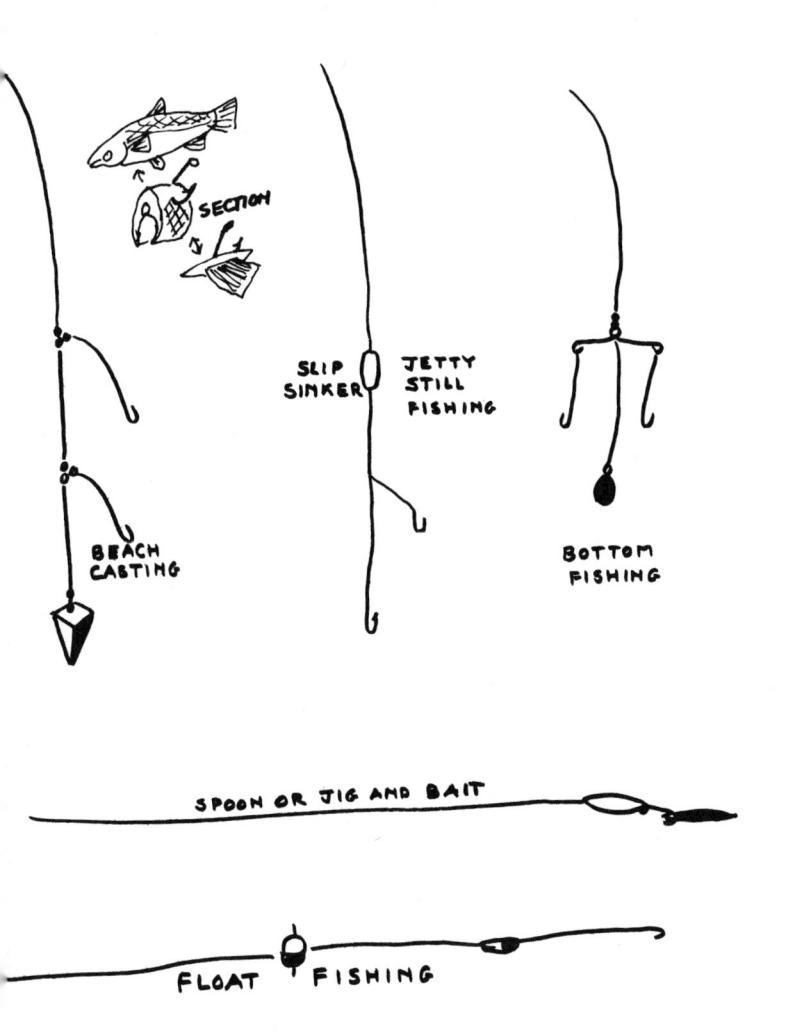

Typical terminal tackle for beach and jetty fishing.

find that whether in a boat or fishing from the land, both methods will produce. Also, quite often, waves and weather prohibit all but the brave (and sometimes the too-daring), fishermen from boat fishing. Rough water and fierce winds can be too much to bear even if there is some possible shelter in the lee of protruding rocks. Still it is in such weather, particularly in northern areas, that the fishing may be tops.

The troller has the theoretical advantage of being able to cover more fishing territory in less time than the angler who wanders up and down the beach or clambers over the rough rocks of a jetty. Certainly, "fish hunting" is better done by trolling. Casting from the shore is more of a waiting game. To troll successfully the angler must as always be aware of the tide, how each hour affects the local waters, how the currents bring in the bait, how the wind crosses up the surface of the water. Watch the sky for the presence of sea gulls feeding on the surface, for this signifies action underwater. The big fish are schooling up the bait, driving them to the surface and the gulls are snatching their share. Also watch for approaching squalls.

Trolling rigs are basically simple. Drift trolling can also involve using the bobber and is particularly effective alongside a jetty right in the mouth of an inlet. Drift fishing is also productive near the surf when a long pool of water inside a sandbar is seen to contain roving big fish chasing smaller ones swept into the "pool".

If the bottom is full of rocks, try to keep the bait above them by adjusting the weight-boat-speed ratio. If the bottom is sandy, troll deeper.

Most jetty and beach trolling is done from relatively small boats. This argues for keeping a sharp "weather eye" peeled. As to the tackle, set the reel drag to well under the breaking

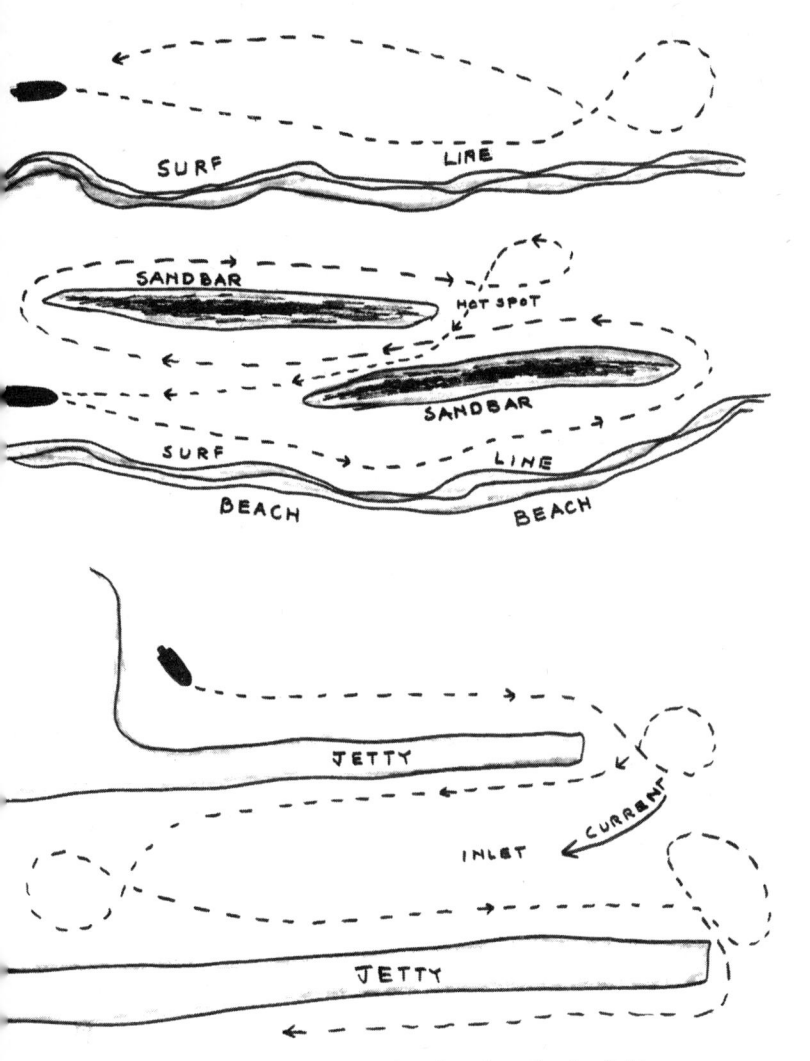

More suggested trolling courses for close-in saltwater fishing.

strain of the line. Tighten it later after a strike. When fishing whole baitfish it is best to allow the line free drag so the game fish has time to mouth it a bit. Then when he has decided to run with it—strike!

Never troll with the rod unattended. Even if it is set into the rod holder, make sure that everything is free, that the line is always uncaught in the guides and that other gear aboard is well away from sudden action. If the rod is hand-held, make sure fingers are well away from the line. Set the reel's anti-reverse so that the handle will not spin on strike or in case the weights become snagged. If two lines are being trolled and a fish hits one of them, the other must be reeled in quickly to avoid a possibly bad tangle. Have the net or gaff ready and the oars and other gear out of action's way.

While fighting a fish, keep a watch so that the boat is not carried into a dangerous tide rip, or pushed up on a rock ledge. Keep alert for other boats. They should keep their distance, but don't depend on it. Watch also for heavy wakes from any passing boats.

If two are fishing, one can man the motor and guide the boat according to the conditions. Then they can take turns fishing.

The training acquired here fishing along the shore is a good rehearsal for the big game show to be experienced out on the open ocean, well offshore and away from the safety of sheltered waters.

12

Offshore Trolling for Big Game Fish

THIS IS BIG time angling for glamour fish found in ocean depths. Some anglers consider it less sporting and less fun than fighting smaller fish on lighter tackle—a bonefish a greater thrill than a 700-pound tuna, for example. But others are consumed with the idea of breaking world records and love the idea of battling a powerful fish three times their weight for hours on end.

Still, good choices can be found fishing for lightweights of this kind in offshore fishing and the heavies. Offshore fishing does not necessarily mean that all the fish have to be big. There is plenty of fun and sport, for instance, in catching a 20-pound king mackerel on 5-pound test line with medium-weight freshwater spinning rod and reel. And it will take time and skill to boat it; the same is true for a 35-pound sailfish or wahoo. There's plenty of thrill also in taking a 40-pound school tuna on light tackle, perhaps more so with light gear than in taking a 700 pounder with the winch-like tackle required for such giants of the sea.

Striped bass, bluefish, cobia, amberjack and, off the Pacific Coast, the yellowtail and several species of smaller tuna will fill the small-to-intermediate bill for deep water light tackle fishing. The big bottom fish, like the jewfish or grouper, will run up to 200 pounds. Catching them offers much long-term steady pull. When it comes to shark, that's something else again. Here the fisherman is up against brawn, tenacity and more excitement than some anglers ever find with the big black, blue-and-white marlin or giant bluefins. So the choice is wide and so are the methods.

Equipment-wise, gear can vary from heavy freshwater items to the heaviest of the saltwater gear complete with a fighting chair in a cruiser cockpit. Boat-wise, it varies from using a twin-engined outboard skiff for quick runs out and back to luxurious 26-foot to over 40-foot cruisers.

Of course, the fisherman does not have to have access to these private boats. There are plenty of party boats that take up to 100 anglers for half and full-day trips. At certain seasons, these boats also fish at night, or right around the clock. Bait, terminal gear, rods and reels are furnished. All the patrons do is bait the hook, throw it overboard and catch fish! The skipper knows where and when the fish are biting and everybody aboard has fun.

Rented outboards and inboards can be obtained at most coastal fishing centers by the day, week or month—even by the entire season. Many anglers who want to fish during a great deal of their vacation period hire a guide and his craft for the whole time.

The formal charter boats are the big ones for long, fast, safe trips to waters well offshore. These craft are seaworthy and capable of operating through storms and sudden blows. Many are equipped with cabins where all necessities and meals can be served. They have plenty of cockpit space for action. The catch is iced and cleaned, or may be turned over to the captain, unless of trophy significance.

Their skippers supply tackle, bait and chum and prefer theirs be used. The crews rig the terminal baits and prepare them for hooking; particularly trolled whole fish that require special preparation in order to ride correctly in the water. Their reputations depend upon the catches. There's competition between boats, whether party or charter and if possible, one should engage such a boat or make his reservation months ahead of the prime season to be sure of spending his fishing time with the best guides and skippers. Usually this pays off in the end, even if it means paying premium prices.

Terminal Tackle for Offshore Fishing

Use bottom tackle or trolling and drifting tackle as usual and slightly heavier tackle if after the big fish. The difference in this kind of fishing from that of the inshore variety is that most trolling will be done with the baits riding directly on the ocean surface.

In most cases, with the exception of trolling for bluefish and stripers in their class, the baits are kept up on the surface but out of the boat's wake by outriggers—long poles angled outward from the craft. Once the terminal rig is set up, the fishing line is attached by means of a clothespin to another line extending over a small pulley at the top of the outrigger and down to the cockpit. By this means the fishing line is then hoisted so that it extends from the reel to the top of the outrigger. The cruiser is started and the baits are allowed to drift and skip along the ocean surface as the boat moves along at appropriate trolling speed. When a fish strikes, the line is jerked from the clothespin and the fisherman's battle is underway. Until this happens, he can do but little except sit, watch, wait and hope. There's a thrill in seeing a marlin, for example, as it approaches sometimes from way behind the bait. He sneaks up on it, makes several passes at it, etc., before finally coming in for the kill.

Rigging the bait to the hook for this kind of fishing is an art that few anglers ever learn or really need to learn. The bait, be it a bonefish, bluefish, or a lesser species such as the flying fish, is opened up, the backbone removed in most cases, and the hook is sewed into the fish in such a way that it will remain vertical when towed as bait. It will flash and wobble more naturally this way and must not be allowed to spin on the line. Those big fish are very choosey!

Other baits are cut fish for drifting and bottom fishing; squid or strips of most any fish available.

Much of deep sea sport fishing and trolling involves chumming. Before setting out for the fishing area, the boat is loaded with several containers of mashed-up menhaden, herring or other bait or trash fish, including the innards of dead sport fish mashed to form an oily, stew-like mess. When the fishing grounds are reached and the course, current and drift are established, the mate scoops out dipper-fulls of the chumming bait, tossing them overboard at regular intervals in the hope of drawing fish to the area and the baits to be trolled. Hence the anglers fish in the chumming "slick". In general, chumming is effective and widely-practiced in offshore fishing. It has been virtually traditional in deep sea fishing for many, many decades; for that matter, perhaps even for centuries.

EQUIPPING FOR BIG GAME FISHING

First comes the boat—a cabin cruiser of from 28 to 40 or more feet; twin-engined; plenty of cockpit space; a forward cabin for rest and shelter; electronic equipment for safety, fish and depth-finding.

Then the tackle is aboard for whatever species is sought. Fighting chairs are needed, usually a pair mounted on the floor of the cockpit. These revolve in a circle somewhat like a barber chair so the angler is always in line with his fish. (When the boat needs to be moved still further in any direction, the skipper, watching the show from his perch above the cabin roof, makes the necessary angulations and speed changes.) The fighting chair has a circular hole for the rod butt. The fisherman wears a harness (of which there are several versions) which can be fastened to each side of the reel. In fighting a large fish, this helps distribute the strain to back and shoulders, as well as arms and legs. The rod holders are usually mounted on the sides of the gunwales and are used for storage and also in fishing if more than the chair rods are used at the same time.

A flying gaff is a very necessary instrument and its barb is to be sunk home into the fish when the mate grasps the leader with his gloved hands preparatory to landing the fish. An assortment of nylon lines (ropes) are needed sometimes to put a loop around the head and tail of the fish, especially if it is a billfish or shark. As stated, a flying bridge or tuna tower are necessities when trying to locate and later maneuver the boat when a giant is on the line. From his elevated position up there the skipper can see over the swells or chops and survey the water for quite a long distance when seeking fish. Outriggers, bait storage cans for bait and chum, long-handle and heavy-duty gaff and gin pole are needed, the last serving often in towing or hoisting a large trophy.

FISHING TACKLE AND TERMINAL GEAR

Since interest runs high with both skippers and anglers for trophy and prize-winning fish, contest regulations applicable to big game fishing and tackle are closely adhered to by all deepwater salts. Some lucky fisherman might hook into a big prize-winner or world's record fish the first time out, and it would be a pity if his tackle were not "regulation." Of course, it is not necessarily the biggest fish that counts, but the biggest taken on specifically weighted and measured gear. This is all set up by the International Game Fish Association, a world-wide clearing house for records.

The big-game reels used are marked in sizes from 1/0 to 6/0. They are manufactured by excellent companies such as Ocean City, Penn, Fin-Nor and Garcia, to mention but a few. These are perfectly designed for heavy fast-running and jumping fish. They are built to stand off terrific pressures.

Lines and their capacities as recommended by the manufacturer are based on thread sizes as previously mentioned. The I.G.F.A. recognizes only 3, 6, 9, 15, 24, 39 and 54-thread lines and their strength is judged when wet. Experts agree that braided nylon or dacron is just about impervious to deterioration in salt water, but these lines do have a good deal of stretch, some more than others, which is a hindrance in some situations. On a long line, their hooking qualities, due to this stretch, are less predictable than is the case with linen lines.

Rods also have a system of classification according to the weight of the tip section. They range from 4 to 36 ounces. For example, take the combination of a correctly balanced set-up. A 9/12 outfit requires a rod with a tip of 9 ounces which will work best with 12-thread line testing at 36 pounds. For such a combination, the correct reel for most conditions will be a 4/0.

Suggested Balanced Tackle Combos

It would be quite impossible and unnecessary to catalogue each and every well-balanced tackle combination here, but five have been selected to cover the range of sizes deemed most practicable.

16/24 Heavy Tackle

Rod: 6 feet, 9 inches overall length.
Tip: Not less than 5 feet. Weight, 16 ounces.
Line: 24-thread, 72 pounds, wet.
Leader: 15-foot length; no limit re strength.
Reel: No restrictions; usually 4/0 to 9/0.

9/18 Medium Tackle

Rod: Length 6½ feet.
Tip: 5 feet. Weight, 9 ounces.
Line: 18-thread, 54 pounds, wet.
Leader: 15 foot; no weight restrictions.
Reel: Usually 4/0 to 6/0.

6/9 Light Tackle

Rod: 6 feet.
Tip: Not less than 5 feet. Weight 6 ounces.

Butt: 18 inches.
Line: 9-thread, 27 pounds, wet.
Leader: 15-foot; no strength restrictions.
Reel: Usually 3/0 to 4/0.

4/6 Light Tackle

Rod: 6 feet.
Tip: Not less than 5 feet, weight 4 ounces.
Butt: Length, 18 inches.
Line: 6-thread, 18 pounds, wet.
Leader: 15-foot; no test restriction.
Reel: Usually 2/0 or 3/0.

3/6 Light Tackle

Rod: 6 feet including butt; 6 ounces in all.
Tip: 5 feet in length.
Butt: 12 inches.
Line: 6-thread, 18 pounds, wet.
Leader: 15-foot: no weight restriction.
Reel: 2/0 or 3/0.

Hooks

Certainly there is a specific hook which is best suited because of its design for certain species of fish and made in size that will capture them properly.

Sailfish: O'Shaughnessy 7/0 to 9/0.

School Tuna: 20 to 45 pounds. Sobey 7/0, 40 to 100 pounds; 8/0 or 9/0, O'Shaughnessy.

Check the I.G.F.A. records occasionally for changes in tackle specifications and record fish recorded.

SHARK FISHING

The surf, jetty and even the bay fisherman will encounter sharks when least expected. It is fun when even a supposedly docile sand shark takes hold. The fight is not dramatic, but there will be a lot of pulling and hauling before the fish is exhausted. These are "accident" sharks, the same as those often hooked through chance out on the big deep. Quite often while trolling for anything from offshore striped bass, school tuna or the big marlin and tuna, a shark will be hooked. Chances are, if it is big, it will eventually get away, since hooks used for ordinary game fish will not suffice. The leaders also, being of wire rather than chain, will not always hold a big one.

Sharks will also attack hooked big game fish. They are attracted to the thrashing of the game fish on the hook and, as the fish tires, they move in for the kill—sometimes as many as six or eight of them. Quite often this leaves the fisherman with only the head of his hooked fish, the shark having taken the most of it and departed. Many world's records have been lost this way.

There is, however, the specialized sport of shark fishing. In this, the fisherman deliberately tackles up for the monsters, using the heaviest rod available and the biggest reel with the strongest lines. Then he attaches a shark chain "leader" and a proper hook of a type described earlier. But before leaving for shark-fishing, it's necessary to visit the meat market or a meat-processing plant to obtain gallons of blood. Fish chum, animal guts and meat are useful, too. Quite a makings for the shark's dinner! Once out on the ocean, the sharking specialist starts his chum line, sets his baits in the outriggers, and the day starts. Other necessary equipment includes nylon lines—ropes for looping the head and tail of the shark when it is about to be boated. The boat should have a gin pole, a stout pole attached to the side of the boat, aft of the cabin, but not in the way of open deck areas where fish are hauled aboard. The shark will eventually be lashed to this pole if it is too large to haul aboard otherwise.

Now, a shark unceremoniously takes hold of the bait. Marlin and other fish usually will first follow the bait for a while, being very touchy and aware that it just might not be to their liking. The shark, on the other hand, throws caution to the wind, since he is virtual king of the sea. His strike is not especially shattering. He merely grabs the bait and takes off the moment he hooks himself, unless the fisherman has already set the hook. Most sharks do not do a great deal of jumping, but the hammerhead and the blue are known to go in for surface acrobatics.

Battling a shark can be long and laborious, but it will rarely be as quiet and long-pull a tussle as in the case of the bluefin tuna. When the shark is tired out, the mate readies the flying gaff, clears the deck for action, readies his lines for the loops. As the shark swims by and if the mate assesses it as thoroughly tired, he attempts to place a loop, first over the snout of the shark, and then one over the tail. In the meantime, the fisherman stays in the fighting chair, doing his part. Quite often several tries will go by, the shark merely swimming by for a closer look.

But when the right time comes, the loops are made secure and the gaff driven into its mark. Finally the shark is led around to the gin pole where, by various means devised by the skipper, it is made fast. Its quite a fight!

A word of warning! Don't look for shark trouble unless from a big seaworthy boat that's properly equipped and manned with at least one person who really knows what he is doing! This is a dangerous sport. Sharks have been known to jump right into the cockpit of a boat. If the boat is small, such as an offshore open skiff, they can bash in the transom or smash the rudder and propeller. Once aboard, that seemingly docile shark can come quickly to life and tear up the deck and everything on it. They don't seem to die very fast, even when shot. Actually, there seems to be no proved way to dispatch them promptly and efficiently.

So, don't go out as a tyro adventurer and tangle with sharks. It takes a great deal of knowhow. Despite this, sharking can be a real he-man sport with greater appeal to some than fishing for the usual big game fish. There are even charter skippers who specialize in this sport.

But, until the new shark fisherman has accompanied an experienced one a few times, he won't really have the knowledge and experience as to what is actually needed for the safety of the boat, the equipment and other people on board, should he be tempted to try it on his own.

FOR REFERENCE

Unhooking and Cleaning the Catch

SOFT-MOUTHED FISH MINUS spiney fins are quite easy to unhook and do not usually chafe or cut the hands. The trout is about the only fish that's completely harmless, even though some big trout have rough teeth. A strong word of caution applies to handling all other varieties. The black bass has spiney fins; catfish have sharp spears hidden in their fins. The bite of the bluefish can be not only painful but poisonous! Naturally, keep at a distance when handling sharks, barracuda and other dangerous game fish including the pike and musky.

Netted or gaffed, the fish should be killed as soon as possible. A simple blow on the head where it joins the neck will

UNHOOKING AND CLEANING THE CATCH

suffice for most small fish. Pierce others in the same spot with a sharp knife. Big ones can be shot or clubbed. Do not try to remove a hook from a flopping, thrashing fish. The hazard here is that one could be lacerated by fins or teeth, or get neatly hooked.

Once dead and unhooked, the fish should be cleaned as soon as possible since too long a delay renders the catch unpalatable. Clean fish before they become stiff and dry; it's much easier that way. Place them in a cool spot, preferably near ice and wrapped securely in newspaper or aluminum foil.

For keeping freshly-caught fish alive, use a metal fish stringer with safety-pin clips. Hook the fish through the lower lip, but *do not hook a fish through the gills or both lips* as this will prevent it from breathing freely and it will probably die. Place the fish into the water, but remove it before moving on; submerge it when stopped.

When deciding whether or not to enter a good saltwater trophy in contests, consult the International Game Fish Association charts and specifications which are frequently revised. They are to be found in some of the bait and tackle shops in popular saltwater fishing ports; if not, they may be obtained by writing The Secretary, I.G.F.A., DuPont-Plaza Building, 300 Biscayne Boulevard Way, Miami, Florida 33131.

Dictionary of Natural Baits

THROUGHOUT THIS BOOK are references to natural baits. In most cases, the baits are common and readily available. But they do not constitute the entire list of natural baits available. Here is a more complete catalogue of natural baits according to category. In the freshwater section, aquatic insects, minnows and small fish, then items such as frogs, toads, salamanders, clams, and crawfish. In the saltwater section there is a greater bait selection. Categories include crustaceans, worms, bait and small fish, shellfish, squid and shrimp.

STREAM AQUATIC INSECTS

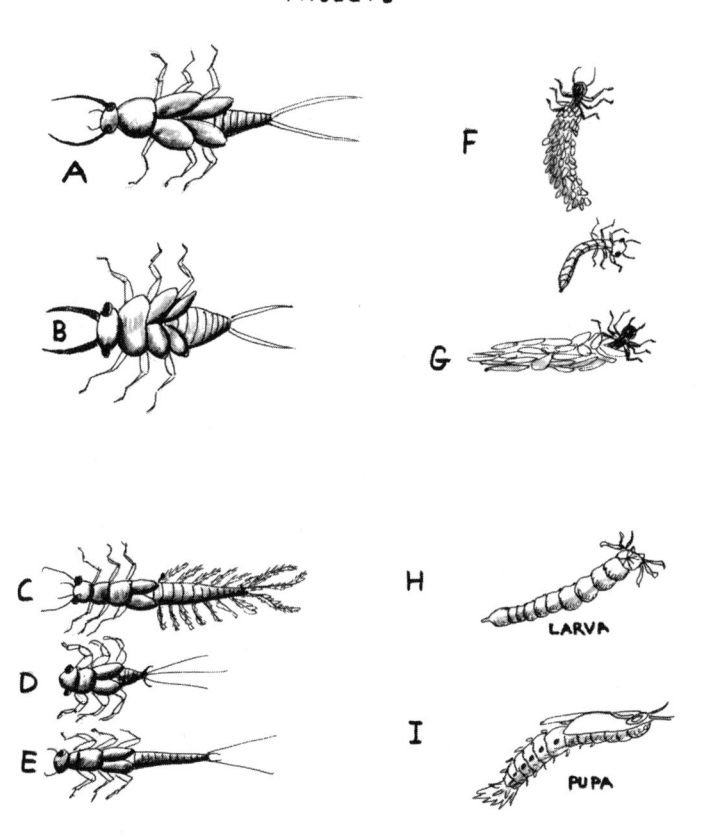

A—Stonefly nymph, one of several small species; B—Giant stonefly nymph; C—Swimming-type mayfly nymph; D—Clinging-type mayfly nymph; E—Clam-boring-type mayfly nymph; F—Caddis fly larva in sand case; G—Caddis fly in leaf-type case; H—Cranefly larva; I—Cranefly pupa.

LAKE AND RIVER AQUATIC INSECTS

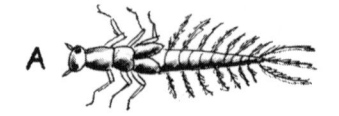

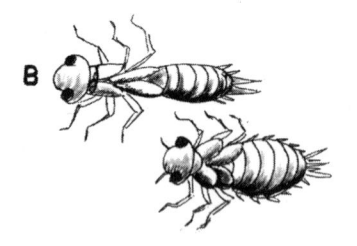

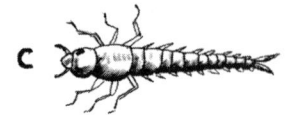

A—Large lake mayfly nymph; B—Dragon and damsel fly larva; C—Hellgramite.

STREAM MINNOWS AND SMALL FISH

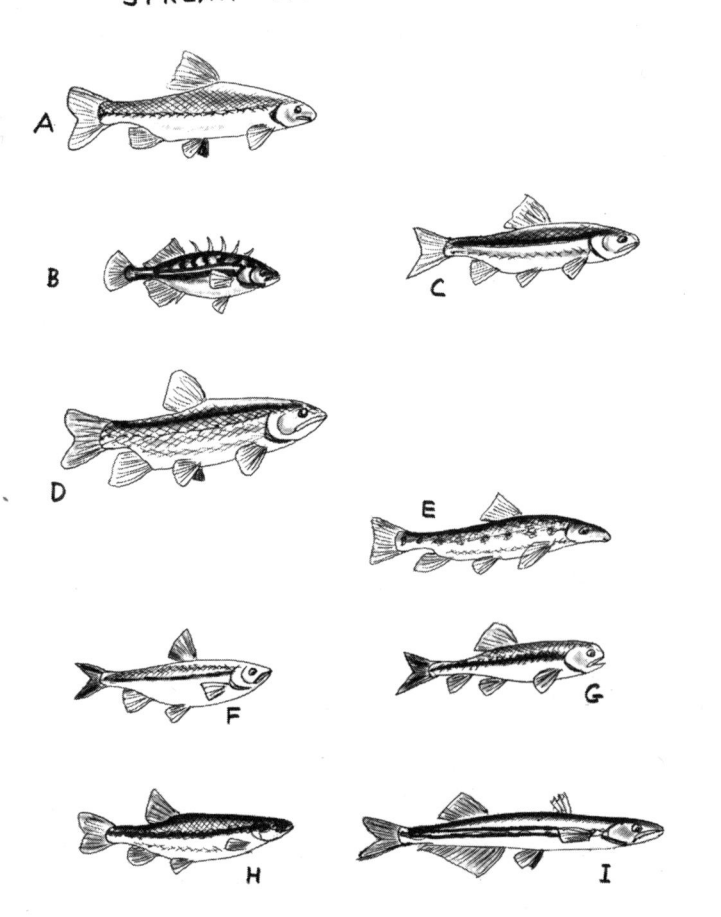

A—Suckermouth minnow; B—Brook stickleback; C—Creek chub; D—Fallfish; E—Torrent sucker; F—Silvery minnow; G—Bluntnose minnow; H—Blacknose dace; I—Brook silversides.

LAKE AND RIVER BAITFISH

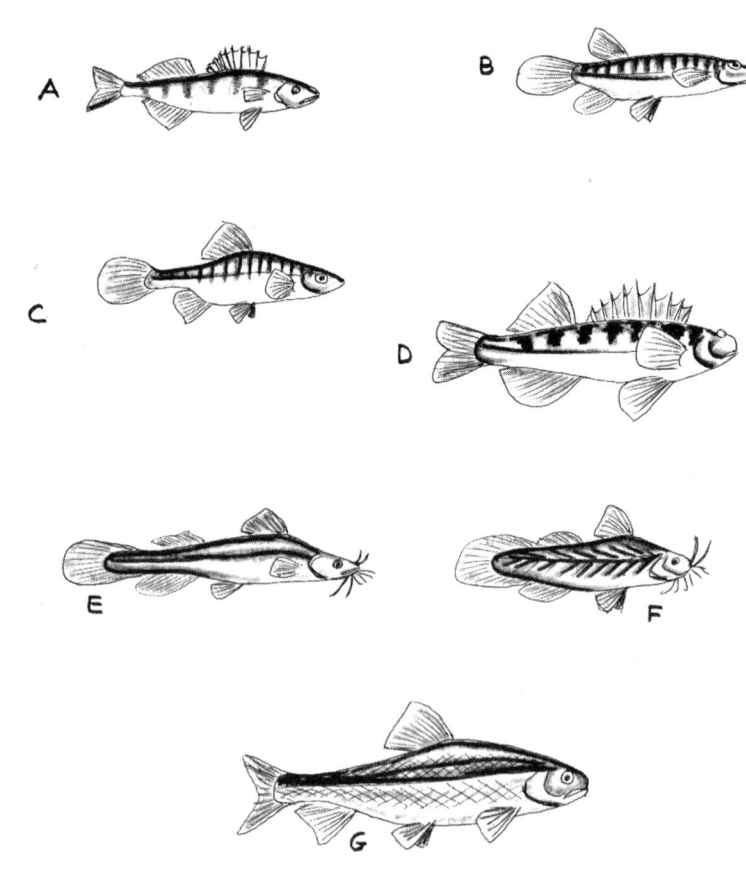

A—Sauger; B—Starhead top minnow; C—Banded killfish; D—Darter; E—Stone catfish; F—Tadpole mad-tom; G—Common shiner.

SOME LAND-BRED INSECTS

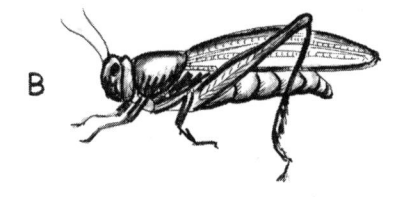

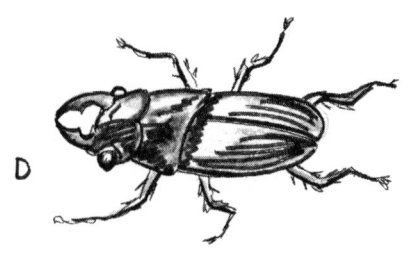

A—Field cricket; B—Grasshopper; C—Typical caterpillar; D—Typical beetle.

ANIMAL BAITS

A—Mouse; B—Frog; C—Crayfish; D—Salamander.

SALTWATER MINNOWS AND SMALL FISH

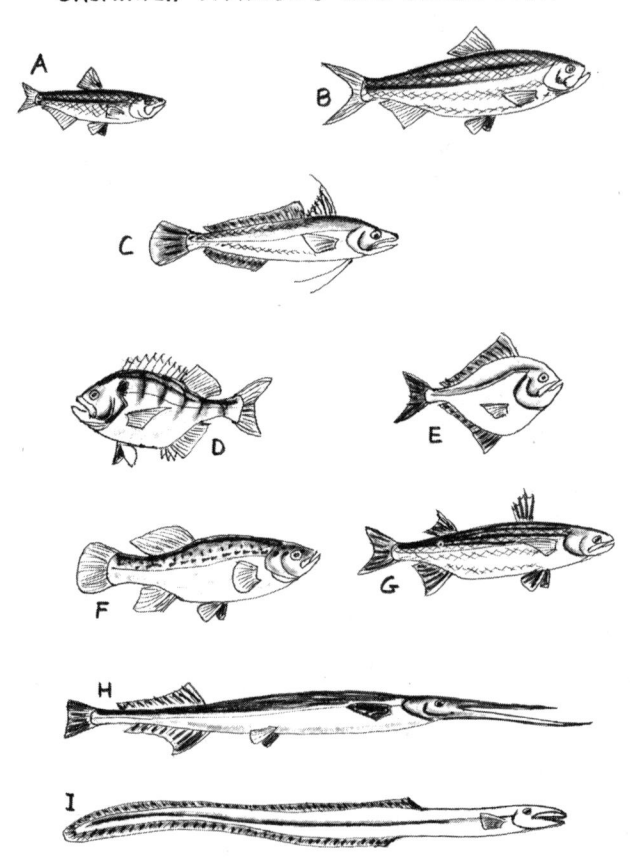

A—Anchovy; B—Glut herring; C—Mud hake; D—Pin fish; E—Butterfish; F—Mummychog; G—Mullet; H—Needlefish; I—Eel.

SHRIMP, CRABS, SHELLFISH, WORMS

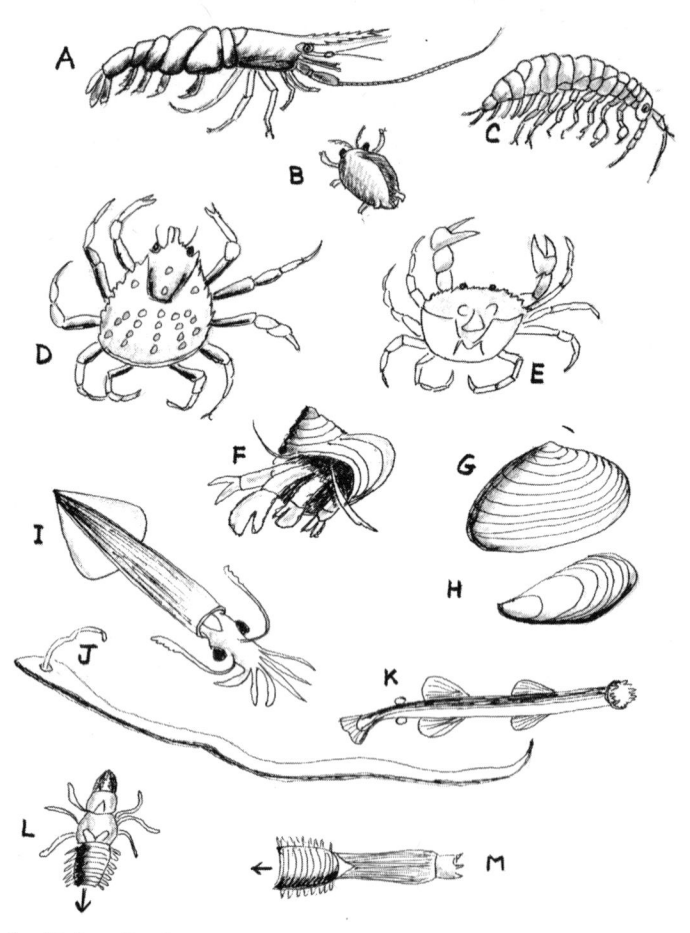

A—Shrimp; B—Sand flea; C—Seaweed hopper; D—Spider crab; E—Green crab; F—Hermit crab; G—Clam; H—Mussel; I—Squid; J—Pink sand worm; K—Arrow worm; L—Clam worm; M—Bloodworm.

Glossary

AFLOAT   On the water.
AMIDSHIPS   The middle of the boat.
ANCHOR   A heavy forging or casting so shaped as to grip the sea bottom and, by means of a cable or rope, hold the boat in the desired position.
ANTI-REVERSE   The mechanism on a reel which allows line to be pulled from the reel while the handle remains still.
AQUATIC INSECTS   Those born in stream or lake and which later fly.
BACKLASH   Line rolling over itself backwards due to the reel overspinning.
BOW   The forward part of the boat.
BAIT FISHING   Fishing with natural foods rather than artificial.
BAIT CASTING   The casting of plugs, lures and baits; a type of tackle.
BALANCED TACKLE   Tackle which balances well in hand and performs to the ultimate, all components including the rod being well-matched to each other such as size and weight of line and reel in relation to terminal rig, lures used, and all ideal for the fish species sought.
BASS-BUG ROD   A staunch fly rod heavier than the usual trout weight designed to throw heavy, wind resistant fly rod lures.
CHART   A map of a body of water containing necessary piloting information.
CLEAT   A piece of wood or metal with projecting ends to which lines are made fast.
COCKPIT   A well or sunken space in the afterdeck of a boat for work or action space.

CREEL A basket or bag that holds caught fish, most often fashioned of willow or canvas.

DRAG On reel, adjustable to brake the speed of line flow from the reel spool.

FLIES, ARTIFICIAL Those made to represent insects and baitfish.

GAME FISH Designated fish species known for their gamey fighting qualities and those under conservation law protection.

HULL The body of a boat or larger vessel.

KNOT To bend a line. A unit of speed.

LEVEL-WIND MECHANISM Winds the line back and forth evenly on the reel.

NON-MULTIPLYING REEL Single-action; one revolution of the handle to one of the spool.

OFFSET HANDLE Rod handle angled and designed for better handling of the reel.

PANFISH Tasty small fish that can be cooked in a pan.

PUSH-BUTTON REEL A closed-face reel featuring automatic line pickup and release controlled by a push button.

SINGLE-ACTION REEL A non-multiplying reel, usually employed only on fly rods.

SNAP SWIVEL A swivel featuring a snap for tying on sinkers, or other lines and hooks.

STRIKING Pulling sharply on the line against the hit of a fish in order to set the hook in its mouth.

TAPERED LEADERS Lengths of almost invisible monofilament material attached between the running line and terminal tackle, tapered down to a relatively fine end.

TAPERED LINES Lines tapered from thin to thick to thin for balance and casting efficiency.

TERMINAL TACKLE Various items attached to the end of the line or leader such as swivels, hooks, sinkers, spinners, etc.

TROLLING A fishing method in which the bait or lure is dragged behind a moving boat.

ULTRA-LIGHT TACKLE The lightest and sportiest tackle practicable for the fishing conditions and species to be fished for.

WAKE The moving waves, track or path formed behind a moving boat. The wakes of larger or faster boats can be very dangerous to small boats in the vicinity.